To: ....

From: ....

Date: ....

OF THE LORD IN SONG:

THE PSALMS

The Remedy

OF THE LORD IN SONG:
THE PSALMS

TIMOTHY R. JENNINGS, M.D.

Published by Lennox® Publishing
PO Box 28266 Chattanooga, TN 37424, U.S.A.

in conjunction with

No portion of this book may be reproduced, stored in a retrieval system,
or transmitted in any form or by any means — electronic, mechanical, photocopy, recording, scanning or other,
except for brief quotations in critical reviews or articles — without the prior written permission of the publisher.
This title may be purchased in bulk for educational, business, fund-raising, or sales promotional use.
For information, please e-mail **requests@comeandreason.com**

Cover design and graphics: Dean A. Scott, mfa
Editing and layout: Mirra Huber

Printed in U.S.A.
March 2020

Library of Congress Control Number: 2019914899
ISBN: 978-0-9858502-8-9

The Remedy of the Lord in Song: The Psalms
Author: Jennings, Timothy R., 1961–

1. Bible, Psalms

TABLE OF PSALMS

PREFACE TO THE PSALMS

In 2016, *The Remedy New Testament Expanded Paraphrase* was released. In the Preface of that volume, I documented the process of Christian thought being infected by the idea that God governs like Caesar—imposing rules enforced by punishment. The traditional view has been that God's law functions in the same way as imposed human laws—which would require God to punish the perpetrator for breaking His rules—rather than recognizing God's laws as design laws—the protocols upon which the Creator built reality to operate. This view has led to the penal/legal theological constructs of Christianity, giving birth to the notion of a punishing god requiring legal appeasement. When translators—despite all innocence of motive—approach the text with this worldview in mind, they all too often bring this legal distortion of a punishing god into the translation.

Additionally, a single Hebrew word can be translated into multiple various English terms, frequently over one hundred, leaving the decision as to which is the most suitable one, to the translator's discretion. This practice opens itself to the biases of the translator.

While paraphrasing the Psalms, I have discovered that the Hebrew language is much more susceptible to the biases of the translators than the Greek. This is because the Hebrew is much more removed from our modern language, and there are many words in the ancient text that scholars have little or no understanding of. Repeatedly, the lexicons note, "Hebrew unknown" or "Hebrew not clear."

Please understand that I believe that the various standard Bible translations are done by good-hearted people giving their honest best to deliver the most accurate translation possible. Unfortunately, they are still subject to their own biases, preconceived ideas and premises—just as I am. My premise is that God is the Creator, operating upon the principles of His grand law of love and expressing His love to all creation by establishing and putting into practice natural/design laws, upon which reality is constructed to operate. Because of Adam's choice, humankind is out of harmony with God's design and is therefore in a terminal state—"dead in trespass and sin." Nevertheless, God, through Christ, has been working to heal and restore all who trust Him, back into unity with Him; back into harmony with His design laws—His original design for human life.

Finally, in the Psalms, poetic license is taken by the original author. Many Hebrew words are used poetically (symbolically or metaphorically), thus adding another layer of interpretive license.

Consequently, within the Psalms, even among non-controversial translations, there are wide differences in translation. Here are a couple of examples:

PSALM 29:9

The Good News Bible: *The Lord's voice shakes the oaks and strips the leaves from the trees while everyone in his Temple shouts, "Glory to God!"*

English Standard Version: *The voice of the Lord makes the deer give birth and strips the forests bare, and in his temple all cry, "Glory!"*

PSALM 32:3,4

The Good News Bible: *When I did not confess my sins, I was worn out from crying all day long. Day and night you punished me, Lord; my strength was completely drained, as moisture is dried up by the summer heat.*

English Standard Version: *For when I kept silent, my bones wasted away through my groaning all day long. For day and night your hand was heavy upon me; my strength was dried up as by the heat of summer.*

King James Version: *When I kept silence, my bones waxed old, through my roaring all the day long. For day and night thy hand was heavy upon me: my moisture is turned into the drought of summer.*

The Remedy: *When I held onto my guilt and shame, refusing to talk to God, I stressed myself and my body decayed, because every day I screamed, "no!" denying the truth. But day and night your healing hand pressed firmly upon me; my resistance evaporated like water in the summer heat.*

In the process of creating a paraphrase, the importance is not so much on being a language expert (as many lexicons and language databases are readily available) but on understanding the subjects of the nature of the war between Christ and Satan (2Cor 10:3-5), God's design-laws, and His character of love.

Without understanding these essential truths, the bias of human law (based on imposed rules) and the subsequent distortion of God (portraying Him as a dictator) get artificially woven into the translation, and thus misunderstanding is perpetuated.

The foremost intention of this paraphrase is to make the concepts of God's design-law, His character of love and His healing truth more accessible to people, in the hope that everyone may come into a personal, saving relationship with our amazing Creator God!

Timothy R. Jennings

x

PSALM 1
DELIGHT IN GOD'S METHODS

1   Happy and healthy are those
        who refuse to listen to the selfish
    or practice the methods of exploitation
        or develop minds that mock God and his designs.
2   Instead, they delight in God's methods and designs (laws);
        they study, adore and internalize his protocols (laws) constantly,
        like day follows night.
3   They are like trees planted by a stream, drawing in life-giving nourishment
        and producing fruit of a godly character that will not wither or die.
        Whatever they do flourishes.
4   But life is not possible for the wicked—
        those that prefer the methods of selfishness!
    They are out of harmony with God's design for life
        and are like dead husks that blow away with the wind.
5   They remain unhealed and will be accurately diagnosed as terminal;
        They will fail to enter into eternal life with the righteous—
        those healed to God's original and right design for life.
6   The spiritually-healthy (righteous) live in harmony with God and his designs
        but the wicked don't: they refuse healing, remain terminal and will perish. ⍰

Psalm 2

Celebrate him with fervor

1. Why are the nations of this selfish world angry at God's character of love?
   Why do their people plot in vain against God's design?
2. World leaders take their stand
   and the rulers unite together
   against the Creator and his design for life,
   and against the One anointed to be our Remedy.
3. They say, "Let us break free from God's design
   and reject God's protocols for life and health."
4. The Creator, who from heaven sustains reality,
   hates their foolishness;
   the Lord knows that heir words don't change reality—
   they're just meaningless noise.
5. He fiercely corrects their misunderstanding
   and persistently assails their false perspectives,
   instructing them,
6. "I have chosen who will reign in Zion;
   my King will rule in sinless perfection."
7. The King will make God's healing plan known:
   God said to me, "You are my Son;
   today my fatherhood to you has become known.
8. Ask me, and I will give you all the nations—
   the entire world will be yours.
9. You will govern them with an unbreakable shepherd's rod of truth and love;
   you will destroy selfishness and crush their ability to coerce and deceive
   like iron crushes pottery."
10. Therefore, worldly rulers, wise up!
    You, who govern the earth, have been warned as to how reality works.
11. So, with humble admiration, live in harmony with God and his designs,
    celebrate him with fervor.
12. Accept the Son with a loving heart lest he let you go
    to die from your terminal condition,
    for he may release you to your choice at any moment.
    Happy and healthy are they who abide in him. ଔ

Psalm 3

From my Creator comes freedom

1 Lord, my enemies are more than I can handle!
    More oppose me every day!
2 They mock me saying,
    "God will not help him."
3 But you, O Lord, are my constant protector from all enemies;
    you remove my fear, heal my mind and glorify my character with your love.
4 I call out to my Creator for help,
    and from his dwelling place he provides all that I need.
5 I sleep well at night;
    I wake refreshed, because the Lord watches over me.
6 I don't live in fear of my numerous enemies
    who sneak around behind me on all sides.
7 Do it now, Lord!
    Deliver me, my precious Savior!
Silence the mouths of my enemies,
    make powerless their biting words.
8 From my Creator comes freedom.
    May your healing love fill the hearts of your people. ❧

Psalm 4

The Lord heals those who trust him

1 You always answer me when I talk to you,
  O Creator who puts right what is wrong in me.
  You heal all my brokenness,
  and now I need your help again.

2 O you selfish people, how long will you lie about me?
  How long will you cling to your fantasies and pursue falsehood?

3 Understand this:
  the Lord heals those who trust him, setting them right with himself;
  he listens when I talk to him.

4 Be passionate, but don't deviate from God's design for life;
  in quiet contemplation search your own heart and apply these truths.

5 Give your heart to God, sacrifice its desires
  and trust him completely.

6 Many people pray, "Can't you make our life better?
  Bless us, O Lord, with good stuff."

7 But you have healed my heart—
  a greater joy than all their material possessions could ever bring.

8 When I sleep, I rest in peace,
  for in your hands alone, O Lord,
  I am perfectly safe. ❧

PSALM 5

I AM RENEWED IN LOVE

1 Hear my words, O Lord,
   but pay special attention to the secret longings of my heart.
2 Hear my voice when I cry out,
   my God and my King, for it is your intervention that I want.
3 Each morning, O Lord, you will hear my voice;
   each morning I will present myself to you
   and eagerly follow your leading.
4 O God, you are not pleased with violations of your design;
   those who insist on death cannot dwell in your life-giving presence.
5 The haughty and proud flee from your presence;
   you hate all deviations from your design.
6 All those who reject the truth and cling to lies will cease to exist;
   the Lord abhors lies and everything that causes eternal death.
7 But I, by your infinite love, am renewed in love to dwell in your house;
   in awe, I will adore you
   and in your holy presence grow in my knowledge of you.
8 Lord, teach me how to live in harmony with your methods and designs
   or my enemies will destroy me;
   make your ways plain for me to understand.
9 The words they speak bring only death;
   their mouths utter only lies about God.
   The poison of lies from the serpent Satan is on their lips,
   because they have accepted his version of God.
10 Diagnose them as terminal, O God!
   Let their false remedy be their doom.
   Let them go, who cling to their sin-sickness,
   for they rebel against your treatment and violate your designs.
11 But all who trust you and follow your directions will be restored to wellness;
   they will sing for joy.
   Spread your healing hand over them,
   that those who love your methods and principles may celebrate in your presence.
12 For truly, O Creator God, you make happy those restored to unity with you;
   your love surrounds them like a shield. ❧

PSALM 6

WRITE YOUR LAW OF LOVE WITHIN ME

1 Talk to me, Lord! Please don't give up on me;
      teach me, but don't be angry with me.
2 I'm so tired, Lord, please grant me your strength.
      O Lord, heal my brokenness, for I hurt deep inside.
3 My heart is heavy; I feel torn apart!
      How long, O Lord, how long must I endure?
4 O Lord, rescue me and restore to me a healthy and holy self;
      heal me—write your law of love within me.
5 I don't want to die—where thoughts cease and I can't think of you—
      I can't praise you from the grave.
6 But I'm dying of grief;
      I can't stop crying:
      all night long the tears soak my pillow.
7 My eyes grieve to see
      that my enemies are those that I love.
8 Depart from me, you whose hearts do not love but are hardened in selfishness,
      for the Lord knows how it grieves me to let you go.
9 The Lord has granted my request,
      he answers my prayers.
10 All my enemies will be ashamed and consumed with fear;
      they will run away confused, disgraced and hopeless. ଓ

PSALM 7

RESTORE YOUR RIGHTEOUS DESIGN WITHIN ME

1 O Lord my Creator, I am only safe united with you.
      Rescue me from the selfishness that pursues me,
2 lest, like a lion, it tears my inner self—my individuality—apart,
      dragging me away from your love, beyond your healing power.
3 O Lord my God, if I prefer sin-sickness—selfishness and fear—
      and I reject your designs of love;
4 if I endanger my friends

by encouraging their selfish enemies,
5   then let my enemies shut me down,
    let them stomp the dysfunctional life out of me
    and let me sleep peacefully in the dust.
6   Let your anger arise, O Lord;
    rise up against selfishness—my worst enemy.
    Intervene now, my God,
    eradicate selfishness—put things right.
7   Bring all humanity back into unity with you;
    reign in their hearts as the God they love and trust.
8   Let the Lord govern all people.
    Govern me, O Lord, restore your righteous design within me;
    restore me completely to your ideal.
9   O God, the source of right—the standard of life and health—
    search our minds and hearts,
    eradicate selfishness, violence, evil—all deviations from your design—
    and those who trust you, immunize from all lies, fear and selfishness.
10 My God—the Creator, Builder and Sustainer of reality—is my protector;
    he heals those whose hearts choose love and truth.
11 My God—the Creator and standard of life and health—diagnoses perfectly;
    he constantly seeks to destroy sin-sickness—
    deviations from His design.
12 If the sin-sick refuse to partake of God's remedy,
    God will sharpen his scalpel—the sword of truth;
    he sets his bow to let them go.
13 He prepares to cease holding their demise at bay—
    to let loose his arrows to destroy the source of pain, suffering and death.
14 Those who allow selfishness to grow within them
    think up self-justifying excuses that deny their terminal condition.
15 Their lies dig themselves in deep—
    deeper into the pit of self-deception.
16 The unhealthy choices they make cause them more injury;
    their persistent selfishness hardens their own hearts.
17 I give thanks to God because his ways are the ways of life and health,
    and I praise the character of the Creator God of love. ✑

Psalm 8
How magnificent is your design of love!

1   O Lord, our Creator,
     how magnificent is your design of love seen throughout all the earth!
   Your design of never-ending giving (the circle of love)
     is written in the cosmos for all to see.

2   From the mouths of trusting children and innocent babes
     comes the foundation of strength—truth and love—
   which distresses your enemies
     and silences your vengeful foes.

3   When I think about the vastness of the universe
     (realizing it is just finger-work for you),
   the moon and the stars,
     which you set and keep in their perfect place—

4   why are humans so important to you,
     or the Son of Man that you care about him?

5   You made human beings just a little lower than God
     but endowed them with glorious Godlike abilities and authority.

6   You designed humanity to rule the planet in love
     like you rule the universe;
     everything on earth you put under their authority:

7   all domestic animals, flocks and herds,
     and all the wild animals,

8   including the birds flying above
     and the fish swimming beneath waves,
     all that lives in the currents of the seas.

9   O Lord, our Creator,
     how magnificent is your design of love seen throughout all the earth! ༒

PSALM 9

YOU ALWAYS DO WHAT IS RIGHT

1 I stand before the universe
   to proclaim with all my heart my adoration for you, O Lord;
   I will tell of your marvelous ways—
   your perfect design of love.
2 In you only do I have life, health and joy;
   before the universe,
   my life is a song revealing your character of love,
   O Creator God.
3 My enemies run from love and truth;
   selfishness and lies disintegrate in your presence.
4 You always do what is right,
   governing the universe in harmony with your design of love.
5 You overthrow the selfish nations and destroy wickedness;
   you permanently eradicate selfishness and lies—
   all deviations from your design.
6 Our enemies cease to exist:
   cut off from you, their cohesion, organization and life disintegrate;
   the names of their gangs, syndicates and institutions will be forgotten.
7 Understand this: The Creator reigns forever;
   from his throne he governs the universe,
   sustaining the laws upon which life is built.
8 He rules the universe in harmony with his character and design of love;
   he will govern with honor and integrity—
   in harmony with his principles of love.
9 The Lord is a sanctuary of healing and safety
   for the battered and abused,
   a fortress of freedom when trapped by life's problems.
10 Those who have personal experience with your character of love
   will trust you,
   for you, O Lord, never abandon those who seek friendship with you.
11 Let your life be a song of love to the Lord
   who governs in perfection;
   tell the entire world the truth about him and his methods of love.

¹² When he carefully procures the remedy, he thinks of the sin-sick;[1]
he does not ignore their cry for help.

¹³ O Lord, intervene in my behalf!
See the pain and suffering that selfishness causes me.
Heal me—save me from my terminal condition—

¹⁴ that my life might reveal that your methods work;
before the entire world
I will celebrate your healing power.

¹⁵ The selfish dig themselves into pits of despair;
their minds are trapped in their own web of deceit.

¹⁶ The Lord has revealed that he governs in love
and always does what is right;
the selfish reap what they sow—doomed by their own choices.

¹⁷ The selfish disintegrate into the soil of the earth—
all those who reject God and his healing remedy.

¹⁸ But those who acknowledge their need of healing
will not be abandoned;
the long-expected restoration of the humble will not fail.

¹⁹ Act now, O Lord, don't let selfishness win;
establish your government of truth and love upon the earth.

²⁰ Humble their hearts, O Lord;
let the selfish world realize they are just mortal beings. ❧

---

1 The KJV renders this: "When he maketh inquisition for blood, he remembereth them" The Hebrew for 'maketh inquisition,' דָּרַשׁ, דָּרֹושׁ [darash/daw-rash], means to carefully investigate or seek. The Hebrew for 'blood' is דָּם [dam/dawm] and has been debated by scholars as to whether this refers to the "life" which is in the blood, or to the "shed blood" resulting in death. Both interpretations are permissible. Taking the perspective that the blood refers to the life—and in this case, the life of Jesus, which is the remedy to our sin condition — I have rendered the phrase as God carefully seeking the remedy while thinking about the sin-sick, those he loves and whom he seeks to save.

PSALM 10
THE CREATOR GOD REIGNS FOREVER AND EVER

1 O Lord, the freedom you have granted is sufficient;
   you have stepped back far enough for us to see.
2 The selfish in their arrogance abuse and coerce the weak,
   but their own hearts are imprisoned by their selfish scheming.
3 The selfish are proud of how they exploit others to get what they want;
   they celebrate thievery and despise the Lord of love and truth.
4 Filled with self-importance, they think God has nothing to offer—
   in their mind, God is irrelevant.
5 They are confident that their me-first way is best;
   your design-laws make no sense to them;
   they ridicule all who are honest and kind—
   those who oppose their selfish ways.
6 They say to themselves, "Nothing can stop us;
   we will succeed in all we do."
7 Under oath they lie and deceive;
   their words inflame fear, selfishness and division.
8 They befriend the unwary;
   without warning they destroy the innocent,
   they covertly hunt for helpless victims.
9 They are predators who sneak in the dark;
   they lurk in the shadows to ensnare the defenseless,
   they snatch the vulnerable and drag them off in their destructive web.
10 Their victims are pulled down and crushed,
   broken by the cruelty of the selfish.
11 The selfish tell themselves, "God doesn't know what we do;
   he can't even see us!"
12 Act now, Lord! Use your healing power, O God;
   deliver the helpless!
13 It's obvious: the selfish reject God.
   They say to themselves, "He doesn't care what we do."
14 But you see all deviations from your design of love,
   diagnosing accurately to heal and restore by your life-giving power.
   The wounded victims trust you with their care;
   you provide for the helpless.

15   Break the power of selfishness and evil;
>   scour out wickedness until there is no more.
16   The Creator God reigns for ever and ever;
>   the selfish nations will disappear from his kingdom of love.
17   O Lord, you have heard the longing of the victim to be whole;
>   you give them hope, because you know their true need.
18   You deliver the helpless and restore the exploited,
>   so that selfishness in human beings may be no more. ⋈

PSALM 11
HE LOVES HARMONY WITH HIS DESIGN

1   I am always safe in God's hands.
>   How can you urge me: "Run to the mountains for a safe hiding place,"
2   just because the selfish draw their weapons, load them,
>   and prepare to shoot from the shadows, without warning,
>   at those who love others and do what is right?
3   When God's design protocols for life—love and truth—are rejected
>   and replaced by arbitrary rules,
>   what can those who love God's designs do?
4   Remember this: The Lord remains in his dwelling place;
>   the Lord reigns from his heavenly throne.
> He watches the descendants of Adam,
>   he examines every person thoroughly.
5   Those who love others he diagnoses as restored to rightness with him,
>   but he hates selfishness and maliciousness;
>   he diagnoses as terminal those who remain selfish.
6   He will unveil his life-giving fiery glory of love and truth upon the selfish—
>   it will be to them like burning coals of torment:
> they experience reality—
>   the Spirit of love and truth burns out selfishness and deceit.
7   For the Creator is putting things right—back the way he built life to operate;
>   he loves harmony with his design,
>   hence those restored to other-centered love will live in his presence forever. ⋈

Psalm 12
The promised remedy of the Lord is pure

1 Help us Lord, lest those who are like you in character disappear;
   those who trust you are vanishing from the earth.
2 People tell each other fictional tales about life,
   deluding themselves with false security.
3 O Lord, cut through their lying words;
   expose as false the boastful
4 who say, "What we say determines what is right.
   We can say whatever we want; who will stop us?"
5 The Lord says, "I will act now,
   because the weak are exploited
and those who need help call out.
   I will provide the remedy they so desperately desire."
6 The promised remedy of the Lord is pure—
   purified like silver in an earthen kiln,
   purified to perfection.
7 O Lord, keep our minds and hearts pristine and safe;
   preserve us from the corruption of lies and selfishness,
8 because the selfish are everywhere about us,
   and lies are what people love. ◌

Psalm 13

My Heart Triumphs in Your Remedy

1 O Lord, don't leave me here forever!
  I pray that you turn to me.
2 How long must I fight my own thoughts,
  be torn by daily heartache, and endure the ridicule of my enemy?
3 See me, O Lord my God, and talk to me.
  Enlighten my mind lest I rest in death.
4 Don't let my enemy boast, "I have crushed him."
  Don't give the adversary a chance to celebrate my defeat.
5 I have absolute confidence in your never-failing love;
  my heart triumphs in your life-giving remedy.
6 I will sing praises to you, my God,
  for you are always good to me. ෬

Psalm 14

God indwells those who choose him

1 Only the irrational believe in their heart,
    "There is no God."
Their minds are corrupted with lies
    and their characters are selfish;
    there is not one who naturally does good.
2 The Lord looks down from heaven
    at all human beings on earth
to see if there are any that understand reality—
    who understand God's character;
    any who seek God and his methods of love.
3 The entire race has turned away from God—
    they accepted lies about him,
    so their hearts are corrupted with selfishness—
there is not one person who naturally does good;
    no, not even one.
4 Will the selfish never learn how life is designed to function?
    To gratify themselves, they use people like gorging on bread;
    being self-absorbed, they never call upon the Lord.
5 Inevitably, they are dying from fear and insecurity,
    for God only indwells those
    who choose him and his methods.
6 The selfish would like to undermine those who love others,
    but the Lord protects his people.
7 I pray that deliverance from selfishness and healing of God's people
    will be sent from God.
How happy will Gods' people be
    when the Lord restores them to his perfect design! ෴

PSALM 15

WHO MAY RESIDE IN YOUR MAJESTIC PRESENCE?

1   Lord, who may live in your heavenly house?
      Who may reside in your majestic presence?
2   Those who live motivated by love,
      who do what is in harmony with your designs,
      who love and speak the truth;
3   those who refuse to gossip or betray their friends,
      and who would never shame their family;
4   those who find the persistently selfish to be vile and unfit
      but magnify those who love and admire the Lord
      and keep their word even when it hurts;
5   those who lend money to help others—
      not to make more money by charging interest;
      those who cannot be bought to hurt the innocent.
   Those who live like this
      are eternally secure. ❧

PSALM 16

YOU ARE THE SOURCE OF LIFE

1. Protect me, O God,
   > for I have put my life in your hands.
2. I say to the Lord, "You are my Creator—
   > the source of my life and health and everything good."
3. The spiritually-healthy in the land (those who love others)
   > are beautiful people with whom I love to be friends.
4. But those who choose other gods only get worse:
   > their pain, suffering and corruption of mind unavoidably increase.
   I will not worship their blood-thirsty gods;
   > I will not praise them in any way.
5. You, Lord—the source of life—are all that I need;
   > you provide all that I have,
   > you make my future secure.
6. I love what you have given me:
   > from you I have received the most wonderful endowment.
7. I proclaim the goodness of God who teaches me his ways;
   > in the quiet of the night I reflect,
   > and my heart is convicted and grows in the truth.
8. I know that God is before me for all eternity.
   > Because he stands beside me, guarding me,
   > I will not waiver from my mission.
9. My heart rejoices, my mouth proclaims glad tidings,
   > and my body rests in hope,
10. because you will not leave me in the grave,
    > nor will you allow your perfect Remedy to decompose.
11. You will proclaim me as the only way of life,
    > filling me with the joy of your life-giving presence
    > and with the pleasure of living with you forever. ɛꞃ

PSALM 17
I WILL BE SATISFIED TO BE JUST LIKE YOU!

1   O Lord, hear my request to be set right with you;
>> listen to my plea for healing.
> Understand that what I am asking
>> is my heart's true desire.

2   From your assessment let my treatment come:
>> you know what remedy is right,

3   for you have examined the secrets of my heart.
>> You have refined me until no selfishness is found—
>> now I am determined never to speak evil.

4   I live in harmony with your designs—just as you direct—
>> and avoid the me-first ways of the selfish world.

5   I carefully choose your methods—the principles life is built upon;
>> I will not deviate from them.

6   I call to you, Lord, knowing you will answer;
>> draw close to me and hear what's on my heart.

7   Pour out your wonderful love and kindness—
>> your healing power to transform and restore to your ideal
>> all those who seek you to deliver them from selfishness.

8   Lord, you keep your eye on me—watch me closely,
>> but hide me in the shadow of your wings

9   from the selfish who seek to destroy me—
>> from enemies all around who seek to kill me.

10   Their hearts are hard, they have no pity;
>> they brag, boast and blow verbal smoke.

11   They follow me everywhere, sniping and harassing from all sides,
>> seeking any chance to tear me down.

12   They are like lions, stalking me,
>> waiting to tear me to shreds.

13   Act now, O Lord, stand in their way, bring them to their knees;
>> cut me free from the selfish and deceitful
>> with your sword of love and truth.

14   O Lord, by your power deliver me from the spiritually-incurable,
>> from those who are terminal in selfishness—who live only for this world.

May their lives be filled with what their hearts desire.
>   They are satisfied by having their children
>   and leaving their wealth to their descendants.
15 As for me, I will be reborn; in sinless perfection I will see your face:
>   when I awake, I will be satisfied to be just like you! ☙

PSALM 18
HE IS THE SOURCE OF HEALING

1   I love you, O Lord; you are my strength.
2   The Lord unites my will with his, making my resolve rock-solid:
>   he makes me strong and heals my brokenness.
>   God is my solid foundation; I trust him completely.
>   He cleanses my mind, protecting me from lies;
>   he is the source of my healing—my Savior.
3   I call out to the Lord—the source of goodness, love and truth—
>   and he saves me from my enemies.
4   The tendrils of death creep through me;
>   the undertow of selfishness fills me with fear.
5   The grave has hold on me and pulls me down;
>   the chains of death have captured me.
6   In my terminal state I call out to the Lord;
>   I cry out to my God for healing.
>   He hears me from where he dwells;
>   he hears my call for help.
7   The earthly systems shake and shudder,
>   the foundations of the pagan high places quiver;
>   they tremble, because God's passion to heal is fired up.
8   The creative breath of life blew from his nostrils like smoke;
>   the fire of truth came from his mouth,
>   the burning flames of infinite love blazed forth from him.
9   He stepped down to earth from his heavenly dwelling place,
>   he entered into darkness, establishing himself in human form.
10 He came, swiftly flying on the wings of angels;

he appeared by the power of the Spirit.

11 Making humanity his tabernacle, he veiled his glory in darkness
surrounded by amniotic fluid—a dark cloud of water.

12 The light of truth goes forth from him—
a hailstorm of fiery truth, powerful like lightning.

13 The Lord spoke truth like thunder from heaven;
the Creator voiced words that burned like fire.

14 His sends out his arrows of truth broadly across the earth—
great flashes of light that only confuse those who prefer darkness.

15 When you rebuke selfishness, O Creator God,
when your nostrils breathe out your life-giving power of love,
the channels of water that bring life are seen,
the foundations that you built life upon are understood.

16 He reached down from heaven and rescued me;
he saved me from drowning in selfishness.

17 He rescued me from my powerful enemy—
from hatred which was too strong for me.

18 These destructive emotions pounce on me when I am down,
but the Lord holds and strengthens me.

19 He brought me out in the open—on display for all to see;
it was his pleasure to strengthen me.

20 The Lord rewards me because I live in perfect harmony with his designs;
because my work shows clearly God's character and methods,
he restores me.

21 I have lived life the way God designed:
I have not chosen selfishness—I have not betrayed my God.

22 All of his plans and designs are before me;
I have not changed any of his protocols.

23 I am flawless—without any defect—before him;
I have kept myself from any wrong—from deviation from his design.

24 The Lord restores me because I cooperate with his treatment plan,
living clean and pure under his supervision.

25 To those who follow your methods you prove you're reliable;
to those who love truth you prove you are innocent.

26 To the purified you show you are the purifier,

but you wrestle against those who twist your design.
²⁷ You heal those who submit to your treatment;
    you will destroy self-sufficiency and pride.
²⁸ You are the light of my life, O Lord;
    my God, you enlighten my darkened mind.
²⁹ With your strength I am quick to overcome obstacles;
    with my God I can surmount life's roadblocks.
³⁰ God's ways are perfect—
    the word of the Lord heals and restores;
    he shields the minds of all who trust in him.
³¹ For who is God other than the Creator?
    Who is the foundation of reality except our God?
³² Only the Creator God equips me with a noble character and a healed mind,
    making my journey through life blameless.
³³ He gives me confidence like a sure-footed deer,
    he enables me to stand on mountain peaks.
³⁴ He teaches me how to wage spiritual warfare
    to demolish impure weapons of lies and selfishness by my sacrifice.
³⁵ You have appointed me the shield of salvation,
    and your power sustains me;
    your humble condescension makes me thrive.
³⁶ You expand my understanding of your ways,
    so that I don't stumble and fall.
³⁷ I pursue my enemies—the infection of lies, fear and selfishness—
    and remove them;
    I don't stop until they are all destroyed.
³⁸ I shatter them with truth and love so that they will never rise again;
    they fall and I stand victorious over them.
³⁹ You equip me for battle;
    you cause all my enemies to bow down before me.
⁴⁰ You allow my enemies to run away—
    those who hate love, to cut themselves off from life.
⁴¹ They beg for help but reject the remedy,
    so there is nothing left to save them;
    they cry out to the Lord, but he has nothing more to say.

42   I annihilate them like dust blown away by the wind;
        I sweep them out of my kingdom like dirt in the street.
43   You have delivered me from the attacks of the selfish;
        you have made me the head of humanity:
        people who were not my subjects are now loyal to me.
44   As soon as they hear the truth about me, they follow me,
        but those not of my kingdom are afraid of me.
45   Those not of my kingdom wither and fade away;
        abandoned to their own terminal condition, they are consumed with fear.
46   The Lord is the fountain of life! Praise to my unshakable Savior!
        Proclaim the greatness of the God who heals me!
47   The one true God purges all defects from his design,
        so that humanity lives humbly under my rule.
48   O Lord, you deliver me from my enemies;
        exalt me above those who hate me,
        and rescue me from violent people.
49   Therefore I will reveal the truth about you before all humanity, O Lord;
        I will sing the beauty of your character of love.
50   He amplifies the victory of his chosen King;
        he constantly pours infinite love upon his chosen One—
        on David's descendant, forever. ◌

PSALM 19

THE DESIGN-LAW OF GOD IS PERFECT

1   The heavens declare God's character and design of love;
        the expanse of nature reveals how he works.
2   Every day they speak the truth about God's methods and principles;
        every night they reveal the knowledge of God.
3   They don't speak in words or text—
        no spoken language is heard.
4   Yet their voice of truth has been proclaimed to all the earth;
        their evidence to the ends of the world.
      He has placed the sun in its home in the sky;

⁵ it arises like a radiant bridegroom from his honeymoon suite
and runs its course eagerly—like a zealous athlete.
⁶ The sun rises at one horizon
and always completes its circuit to the other;
its light shines as a witness to the entire earth.
⁷ The design-law of God is perfect,
restoring one's life.
The principles of the Lord are constant,
imparting wisdom to those without it.
⁸ The prescriptions of the Lord are right,
bringing happiness to the life.
The protocols of God are brilliant,
enlightening the mind.
⁹ Worship of the Lord heals
and is everlasting.
The decisions of the Lord are always correct
and completely righteous.
¹⁰ They are more valuable than gold,
even much refined gold;
they are sweeter than honey,
even from the honeycomb.
¹¹ They teach those who serve you how reality works—
in living in harmony with them, there is great benefit.
¹² Who can identify every defect in their heart?
Heal everything—even what I cannot see.
¹³ Change my heart—refrain me from selfish choices;
don't let selfishness control me:
then I will be spiritually healthy,
free from deviations from your great design.
¹⁴ Then the words I speak and my inmost thoughts
will be pleasing to you,
O Lord, my refuge and my remedy. ଓ

Psalm 20

May the Lord's Healing Plan Succeed

1 May the Lord answer you when you are in anguish;
    may the character of the Creator God ennoble you.

2 May he strengthen you from his dwelling place
    and sustain you from his holy city.

3 May he preserve the knowledge of your complete selflessness;
    may he confirm as effective
    the remedy of your perfect self-sacrifice.

4 May he give you what your character merits
    and make your healing plan succeed.

5 We will sing for joy when you win—when your remedy is procured;
    we will live proclaiming the character of our God of love.
    May the Lord accomplish all you ask of him.

6 Now I know that the Lord will deliver his Anointed One;
    he answers him from his sinless heavenly home
    with all the healing and saving power of omnipotence.

7 Some try to heal themselves—to win the victory in their own strength—
    but we trust our restoration to the Creator God who is love.

8 They collapse and die in their terminal condition,
    but we rise up and live in eternal perfection.

9 The Lord will deliver our king!
    He will answer when we call! ❧

Psalm 21

Rise up, O Lord, in the full power of your love and truth

1 O Lord, the king delights in the vitality you give.
    He overflows with joy,
    celebrating the restoration you provide!

2 You granted him the regeneration his heart desired
    and have not denied his request for healing.

3 You bring him the costliest gift—
    you crown him with a pure character like the finest gold.

4 He asked for life from you
    and you gave him life eternal.

5 Through your victory over selfishness, his character is ennobled;
    you have restored him to radiant beauty—
    majestic and splendid.

6 You have made him eternally blessed
    with the joy of living in your presence.

7 For the king trusts the Lord;
    through the unfailing love of the Creator God,
    he will not waver.

8 You will vanquish your enemies—fear, selfishness and lies;
    your righteousness will uncover hatred.

9 At the time of your appearing,
    love will burn out all fear and selfishness,
    and truth will burn through lies:
    in your presence, O Lord, they will be consumed;
    your fires of love and truth will devour them.

10 Their fruit of pain, suffering and death
    you will eradicate from the earth;
    the seeds of selfishness you will eliminate from humanity.

11 Although they pervert your design and they lie about you,
    their wicked plans will not succeed,

12 for they will flee from you
    when they face your arrows of truth.

13 Rise up, O Lord, in the full power of your love and truth;
    we will sing praises of your victory! ⊂⊇

Psalm 22

My God, my God, why have you let go of me?

1 My God, my God, why have you let go of me and given me up?
I cry desperately for help,
   but help is far away.

2 My God, during the day I cry to you, but you leave me alone;
   into the darkness I am not silent.

3 You are holy perfection
   and indwell the glory of those who prevail with God.

4 Our ancestors trusted you;
   they trusted and you healed their hearts.

5 They called to you and were transformed;
   they trusted you and you took away their shame.

6 But I don't feel like a Son of God; I feel low, like a worm—
   loathed and reviled by people.

7 Any who see me taunt and scorn me;
   they sneer insults and shake their heads, saying:

8 "He claims he trusts God;
   let God rescue him now!
Let the Lord save him,
   since he loves him so much."

9 You brought me into the world right from the womb;
   you made me feel safe upon my mother's breast.

10 I was dependent upon you from the moment of my birth;
   from the moment I was born you have been my God.

11 Do not stand too far from me,
   for the agonizing ordeal is upon me
   and there is none to help me.

12 Violent men surround me like raging bulls—
   they press in around me like fierce bulls of Bashan.

13 They open their mouths to destroy me,
   tearing me down like lions ravaging their prey.

14 My strength fails, my life-blood drains out like water,
   my limbs are stretched—pulled apart at the joints.

My heart weakens like wax,
    slowly torn apart within me.
15 My mouth is as dry as baked clay,
    my tongue sticks to the roof of my mouth;
    you have set the dust of death on me.
16 The selfish and hateful surround me,
    like wild dogs they close in on me;
    they have pierced my hands and feet.
17 My bones protrude—easy to see;
    my enemies stare in triumph, gloating over me.
18 They divide my garments among themselves
    and roll dice for my clothing.
19 O Lord, don't go too far away;
    O my Source of strength, be ready to help me.
20 Save my individuality from destruction when I die—
    deliver your precious One
    from the power of these wild dogs.
21 Rescue me from the vicious—those like ravenous lions;
    you save me from the beastly—those like wild oxen!
22 I will reveal your character to my brothers and sisters;
    in the presence of humanity I will sing your praises.
23 All you who are loyal to the Lord, spread the truth about him!
    All who with God have prevailed over selfishness,
reveal his character of love!
    Adore him, all you with character like Israel!
24 For he has not reviled or devalued
    the painful victory of his Afflicted One;
he has not rejected him
    but answered him when he called.
25 You are the theme of my praise in the great assembly;
    I will complete my mission to procure the remedy
    for all the loyal to know.
26 The spiritually-hungry will partake of the remedy and be fully healed;
    those who seek God will praise him—

their inner selves (individualities) will live forever!

27 People from around the world
   will remember the God of love and return to him;
   from every ethnic group on earth
   people will worship him.

28 For God is the Creator—the source of life—
   and he governs reality and sustains the laws of nature.

29 All the spiritually-healthy on earth will live with him and worship him;
   all the spiritually-sick and dying will concede that God is right—
   those who are terminal and have rejected God's saving remedy.

30 Our descendants will join his team
   and teach future generations about the Lord.

31 They will spread his healing remedy
   to people not yet born,
   for he has accomplished it. ⌀

PSALM 23

THE LORD IS MY FRIEND—I HAVE EVERYTHING I NEED

1   The Lord is my friend—I have everything I need.
2   He provides rest where I can gather strength,
         he leads me to peace and safety—like still waters;
3   he heals my inmost self.
     He leads me through the process of spiritual restoration
         for the magnification of his character of love.
4   Moreover, when I go through the dark times—
         when I feel like I am going to die—
     I will not give into fear or choose selfishness,
         for you are right there with me;
     your rod of truth and staff of love,
         they comfort me.
5   You provide a feast to nurture me
         in plain view of my enemies.
     You cleanse my mind with the oil of your Spirit;
         my cup of joy overflows.
6   Only goodness and love will follow me
         all the days of my life,
     and I will live in God's heavenly home
         for evermore. ⚮

PSALM 24

WHO IS CAPABLE OF STANDING IN HIS HOLY PRESENCE?

1 The earth *was created by God, and everything in it is his—*
    the entire world and all living upon it;

2 *for he built the land-masses upon deep reservoirs*
    and established life upon flowing waters.

3 *Who is able to enter the Lord's throne-room?*
    Who is capable of standing in his holy presence?

4 *Those who love purely—in action and in heart,*
    who do not embrace false views of God
    or practice deceit.

5 *They will receive healing from the Lord—*
    complete restoration to righteousness from God—their Remedy.

6 *Such purity characterizes those who seek him;*
    who with God overcome, like Jacob.

7 *Look up and unlock the gates to your minds;*
    open the doors to your hearts,
    that the King of Love and Truth may enter in.

8 *Who is this King of Love and Truth?*
    The Lord strong in love and mighty in truth—
    the Lord mighty in battle against lies, fear and selfishness.

9 *Look up and unlock the gates to your minds,*
    open the doors to your hearts,
    that the King of Love and Truth may enter in.

10 *Who is he, this King of Love and Truth?*
    The Lord God Almighty—
    he is the King of Love and Truth! ෨

Psalm 25
Teach me your methods, O Lord

¹ To you, O Lord, I offer my life;
²   it is you that I trust, O my God.
    Save me from shamefulness,
        don't let my enemies—fear and selfishness—
        triumph over me.
³ Shame is not the lot
        of those who learn to trust you,
    but shame and disgrace are the portion for those
        who betray truth and love.
⁴ Teach me your methods, O Lord,
        show me your protocols for life.
⁵ Guide me to live in harmony with your design
        and teach me your principles,
    for you are the God who heals me.
        I put my hope in you every day.
⁶ I remember your unfailing kindness and love, O Lord,
        for they are—like you—eternal.
⁷ Don't think about my past sin-sickness—
        the symptoms of selfishness from my youth;
    think about your loving remedy that heals me
        on account of your goodness, O Lord.
⁸ The Lord is good; he is the standard of life—of what is right;
        therefore he teaches the terminal—
    those out of harmony with his design—
        the way back to life.
⁹ He shows those willing to learn
        the way he created life to be lived;
    he teaches them his methods.
¹⁰ All the Lord's methods are reliable and healing
        for those who choose to live in harmony with them.
¹¹ For the sake of magnifying your loving character, O Lord,
        remove the twisted corruption from within me, though it is great!

12 Those who esteem and revere the Lord,
      he will teach the way they should live.
13 They will have good lives,
      and their descendants will inherit the earth.
14 The Lord is a friend to those who love and revere him;
      he shares his healing remedy with them.
15 I look constantly to the Lord for help,
      for he will set me free from the ties that bind me.
16 Look at me and show me compassion,
      for I am alone in my suffering.
17 Bring peace to my heart,
      free me from my burdens.
18 Examine me closely and see the cause of my suffering,
      and take away all deviations from your design.
19 Look at how many enemies I have
      and how violently they hate me!
20 Protect me and save me,
      don't let me be defeated—
      my safety is only in you.
21 With a mature, Godlike character of love I will be kept safe,
      because my trust is in you.
22 Save those who overcome in union with you, O God,
      from everything out of harmony with your perfect design. ℃

PSALM 26

CONFIRM THAT I AM WELL, O LORD

1 Confirm that I am well, O Lord,
      since I now live in harmony with your design
      and trust in you completely.
2 Examine me and test my motives, Lord;
      diagnose any remaining defects in my desires and thoughts.
3 Your never-failing love is my treatment plan;
      I faithfully follow your methods.
4 I don't join with those whose hearts are devoid of your Spirit;
      I am not friends with those who feign godliness.
5 I hate the company of the selfish
      and won't hang out with the vile and hard-hearted.
6 I maintain my healthy and pure lifestyle
      and continually surrender myself to follow your will.
7 I broadcast my thankfulness,
      telling everyone of your wonderful works of restoration.
8 Lord, I love living with you,
      being glorified by your presence.
9 Do not include me with the terminal
      or with those who refuse your remedy—
10 those who insist on choosing selfishness over love
      while offering payments to buy their salvation.
11 But I live in harmony with your design-laws for life;
      through your grace, heal me completely!
12 I stand on the solid ground of your design;
      in assembled throng of the saved I will praise the Lord. ౪

PSALM 27

THE LORD ENLIGHTENS ME AND HEALS ME

1 The Lord enlightens me and heals me—
    why should I be afraid?
The Lord keeps me safe—
    why should I be afraid?

2 When selfish people attack me and try to destroy me,
    they will stumble and fall.

3 Even if surrounded by an entire army,
    I will not be afraid;
even if the army attacks,
    I will trust the outcome to God.

4 There is one thing I desire from the Lord;
    one thing my heart truly wants:
to be part of the Lord's family and live in his house all my life,
    to gaze upon his beauty, to have him as my teacher.

5 He will shelter me from danger;
    he will keep me safe in his home
    and will establish me, secure, on the immovable Rock.

6 My character will rise above the selfish enemies around me.
    With joy I will offer my heart as his temple;
    I will sing—yes!—I will sing praises to the Lord.

7 Hear my request, O Lord,
    and by your grace, grant my heart's desire.

8 My heart desires to be in your presence,
    so I seek you, Lord—

9 don't hide yourself from me;
    don't say 'no' to my request!
You have always helped me;
    don't refuse to help me now, O my God, my Savior.

10 Even if my father and mother abandon me,
    the Lord will hold me close.

11 Teach me, Lord, how to live your way;
    lead me down healthy paths,
    because enemies watch for opportunity to attack.

¹² Do not leave me to the will of my enemies,
for they spread lies about me and threaten me.
¹³ I know that I will see the beauty of the Lord's goodness in the earth made new—
the land of eternal life.
¹⁴ Trust in the Lord, be strong and confident.
Trust in the Lord. ↩

Psalm 28

The Lord Is the Strength for Those Who Trust Him

1   I call to you, my never-changing, rock-solid Lord;
>don't fail to speak to me,

for if you fail to act,
>I will deteriorate and become nothing—just like those in the grave.

2   Be merciful to me when you hear my voice,
>when I call to you for help,

as I reach out my hands
>to your holy dwelling place.

3   Do not include me with the deceitful and selfish,
>with those who violate your designs for life,

who speak words of love and trust
>but plot evil in their hearts.

4   Give them what their deeds have caused—
>the fruit of their evil work;

give them what their actions have chosen—
>let them reap what they have sown.

5   Because they do not care to understand or value the Lord's design
>or how he runs his universe,

he will overthrow them
>and not restore them.

6   All praise be to the Lord,
>for he has answered my call for help.

7   The Lord strengthens my heart and shields my mind;
>when I trust him with all my heart, I receive help.

My heart overflows with joy;
>I sing songs of thanks to him.

8   The Lord is the strength for those who trust him,
>a sanctuary of healing for all who partake of his remedy.

9   Heal your people and bless those who trust you;
>be their deliverer, and care for them for all eternity. ❧

PSALM 29
ADORE THE CREATOR FOR THE BEAUTY OF HIS CHARACTER

1 Give allegiance to the Creator, all heavenly beings;
      honor the Creator for his beauty and majesty.
2 Adore the Creator for the beauty of his character;
      worship the Creator for the perfection of his being.
3 The voice of the Creator is heard in the rainstorm,
      the power of the Lord is heard in the thunder;
      the Creator designed the many waters.
4 The voice of the Creator is powerful;
      the voice of the Creator is magnificent.
5 The voice of the Creator breaks the cedars;
      the Creator shatters the cedars of Lebanon.
6 He makes the mountains of Lebanon dance like a calf,
      Mount Hermon jump like a bull.
7 The voice of the Lord is creative energy—
      the source of lightning bolts.
8 The voice of the Creator shakes the wilderness;
      the Creator shakes the Desert of Kadesh.
9 The thunder of the Creator bends large trees
      and strips the forest bare.
   All the intelligences in his dwelling place
      marvel at the majesty of the Creator.
10 The Creator overrules the flood;
      the Creator governs as King forever.
11 The Creator gives life to those who trust him;
      the Lord restores them to perfect health. ☙

Psalm 30

The Favor of the Lord is Life

1   I give you all the honor and praise, O Lord,
       for you have saved me,
       preventing my enemies from celebrating my defeat.

2   My Lord and my God, I called to you for help
       and you healed me.

3   O Lord, you pulled me from the grave—
       I was dying and you restored my life.

4   Sing to the Lord, all who have hearts like his;
       be thankful for his character of perfect love.

5   For anger lasts only a moment,
       but the favor of the Lord is life.
    Weeping may come with the darkness,
       but rejoicing comes with the light.

6   When times were good and I felt confident, I said,
       "I can do no wrong!"

7   But Lord, all my success came from you—
       your presence was my mountain-fortress.
    When you let me leave your presence,
       I was overwhelmed with fear.

8   I called out to you, O Lord,
       I cried to you for help:

9   "Death is a rip-off,
       my going into the grave cheats you.
    Will the dust sing your praises?
       Will it spread your truth?

10   O Lord, respond with mercy;
       my Lord, please help me!"

11   You have turned my despair into celebration;
       you have removed my degradation
       and covered me with joy,

12   that my life may be a beautiful song to you
       and not an empty void.
    O Lord my God,
       I will forever give you thanks. ∞

PSALM 31

YOU ARE MY REMEDY

1 O Lord, I come to you for healing:
>   don't let guilt and shame destroy me;
>   restore me to your perfect design.

2 Listen to me—listen closely and heal me—heal me quickly;
>   be my unfailing remedy,
>   a healing sanctuary to renew me.

3 Since you are my remedy and my sanctuary,
>   reveal your character of love by recreating me in your image.

4 Free me from fear and selfishness which have entrapped me,
>   for you are my remedy.

5 I trust you, and I place my life in your hands,
>   for you will cure me—no matter the price,
>   O my Creator—God of reality.

6 I hate the persistent use of false remedies;
>   my confidence is in the Lord alone.

7 I will celebrate and rejoice in your love—your healing design for life,
>   for you saw the misery of my terminal condition
>   and knew the cause of the sickness ravaging my inner self.

8 You have not surrendered me to be enslaved by fear and selfishness—
>   the enemies of your design—
>   but have enabled me to stand free, renewed in truth and love.

9 Pour your healing grace upon me, O Lord, lest I be crushed by guilt and shame;
>   my eyes are swollen from crying,
>   my heart is torn with sorrow and regret.

10 My life is stuck, consumed with guilt—with reliving my mistakes;
>   years I wasted bemoaning the past.
>   I'm exhausted, worn out with guilt;
>   I am getting weaker and weaker every day.

11 My enemies—lies, fear and selfishness—have made me ashamed,
>   my neighbors are tired of my self-loathing.
>   My friends dread to hear more of my constant negativity—
>   when they see me coming, they hide from me.

12 They have moved on, put me out of their minds as if I were dead;
>   I am considered broken beyond repair.

13 I hear criticism in the words of others,
    I am terrified around people:
    they make plots to undermine me and seek to crush my heart.
14 But I put my trust in you, O Lord;
    you are my God!
15 My future is in your hands:
    free me from fear and selfishness—my enemies that constantly pursue me.
16 Immerse your servant in your life-giving glory;
    heal me with your unfailing love.
17 Negate my shame, O Lord, for I call upon you;
    but let the unhealed be consumed by shame—
    may they lie silent in the grave.
18 May the promotion of all false remedies be stopped,
    for the self-sufficient deny reality—
    they scorn God's design for life.
19 Beyond counting are the benefits of your goodness—
    the treasures you have built into reality for all who humbly follow you;
  those who trust you and follow your methods
    reap your blessings, for all the universe to see.
20 You eradicate their sin-sickness by your presence—your secret plan—
    freeing them from the trap of pride and selfishness;
  in your sanctuary you defend them
    from the words of the accuser.
21 All praise and honor be to the Lord
    for the wonders of his unfailing love that rescued me
    when I was besieged by worldliness.
22 Terrified, I cried,
    "I have cut myself off from God!"
  But you heard my plea for mercy
    when I called out to you for help.
23 Love the Lord, all his faithful followers!
    The Lord preserves those who live in harmony with his design,
  but the arrogant, who choose their own way,
    he leaves to reap their full reward.
24 Be strong and confident,
    all you who hope in the Lord. ❧

PSALM 32

I WILL TEACH YOU MY METHODS

1   Happy are they
   whose wicked minds are restored to perfect purity,
   whose selfishness is eradicated.
2   Happy is the person
   whose infected heart the Lord transforms to perfection,
   in whose mind there is no deceit.
3   When I held onto my guilt and shame, refusing to talk to God,
   I stressed myself, and my body decayed,
   because every day I screamed, "no!" denying the truth.
4   But day and night, your healing hand pressed firmly upon me;
   my resistance evaporated like water in the summer heat.
5   Then I admitted my sin-sickness to you
   and did not hide my character-deformity.
   I said, "I will confess my selfishness to the Lord"—
   and you healed me and freed me from guilt.
6   Therefore let all the faithful ask you for this same healing
   while healing is still possible;
   then when the guilt, shame and regrets of life come flooding in,
   the faithful will not drown in them.
7   You are my safe harbor;
   you protect me from the storms of life
   and turn my life into a song of deliverance.
8   The Lord says,
   "I will teach you my methods and how to live in harmony with my designs;
   I will guide you and watch over you.
9   Don't be like the unthinking horse or mule
   that do not reason or understand
   and must be forced by bit and bridle
   to follow the simplest instructions."
10   Many are the sufferings of those who defy your designs,
   but those who trust the Lord
   are healed by his never-failing love.
11   Celebrate God's goodness and be happy, you spiritually-healthy;
   sing for joy, all you with hearts like God's! ❧

Psalm 33

The Design-Laws of the Lord Stand the Test of Time

1   All you with godly character, lift your voices in joyous celebration of the Lord;
      it is beautiful when those restored to God's design praise him.

2   Praise the Lord with the harp,
      make music to him with stringed instruments.

3   With your new heart sing to him a new song,
      play beautifully, and proclaim boldly your joy.

4   For the Lord's design-laws are true—the only right way to live;
      all he does is reliable, constant and unwavering.

5   The Lord loves healthy living—life in harmony with his design;
      all living systems on earth proclaim his unfailing love.

6   The Lord spoke the universe into existence;
      by the life-energy breathed from his mouth
      he formed worlds, moons, and stars.

7   He gathered the waters into seas and lakes
      and created deep ocean-reservoirs.

8   Let the entire earth revere the Lord,
      let the entire human race be in awe of him!

9   For he spoke, and the earth was created;
      he commanded, and it came into being.

10   The Lord eradicates the ways of the wicked world;
      he nullifies the schemes of the selfish.

11   But the design-laws of the Lord stand the test of time;
      the intentions of his heart are eternal—the foundation of eternal life.

12   Happy and healthy are the people whose God is the Lord—
      those who choose to receive the Lord's endowment.

13   The Lord looks down from heaven
      and sees every human being—

14   from his heavenly home he keeps watch
      over all who live upon the earth:

15   he designed the human mind
      and can read the motive of every action.

16   No king triumphs by the strength of his army,
      no warrior survives combat due to his fighting skill.

17 Don't trust your war-horse to save you—
    despite its training and strength, it cannot deliver you.
18 But the Lord oversees the care of those who follow his plan—
    those who trust in his unfailing love
19 to save them from death
    and keep them alive through famine.
20 Our hearts long for the Lord;
    he is our deliverer and protector.
21 Our hearts are healthy and happy,
    for we have trusted in him who is love.
22 May your unfailing love fill us, O Lord,
    for our only hope is in you. ❧

PSALM 34

EXPERIENCE FOR YOURSELVES THAT THE LORD IS GOOD

1 I will praise the Lord at all times;
    I will always thank him and give him the credit.
2 My heart explodes with appreciation of the Lord;
    let the humble hear the good news and join the celebration!
3 Join me and share the goodness of God;
    together, let's radiate his character of love.
4 I sought the Lord, and he answered me;
    he set me free from all my fears.
5 Those who adore him shine brightly;
    their faces are never clouded by shame.
6 The helpless sinners cry for help, and the Lord answers them;
    he heals them from all their sin-sickness.
7 The angel of the Lord stands guard around those who remain loyal to him,
    and he restores them.
8 Experience for yourselves that the Lord is good;
    happy and healthy are those who trust in him.
9 Honor the Lord, you his spiritually-healthy people,
    for those who abide by his methods

have everything they need.

10 Even lions sometimes are hungry and grow weak,
     but those who follow the Lord lack nothing that is good for them.

11 Come, you eager to learn, and listen to me:
     I will teach you the ways of the Lord.

12 Who wants an abundant and full life?
     Who wants a long, healthy and happy life—an eternal life?

13 Then refuse to gossip or speak evil,
     or tell any lie or falsehood.

14 Purposefully reject evil and selfishness and instead choose to do good;
     always seek to heal and bring peace.

15 For the Lord watches over those who live rightly—
     in accordance with his design of love—
     and he hears all they have to say;

16 the Lord works to eradicate evil and selfishness—to heal those infected by it—
     but those who refuse his remedy will be cut off from the earth
     and never thought of again.

17 Those set right with God call to him and he answers them;
     he heals them from all their sin-sickness.

18 The Lord stays close to the grief-stricken and heartbroken
     and heals those who humbly allow him to.

19 Those whose hearts are right with God may have many problems in life,
     but the Lord saves despite life's troubles;

20 he watches over his faithful—keeping them strong like bones—
     they will not be broken.

21 Evil—the willful deviation from God's design—kills the wicked;
     those who hate the godly will suffer its consequences.

22 The Lord heals those who follow his treatment plan;
     no one who trusts in him will ever be lost. ᑫ

PSALM 35

I WILL REJOICE IN THE LORD

1. Neutralize all agents of selfishness that assail me;
       attack and destroy the evil that infects me.
2. Reinforce your breastplate of righteousness and your shield of love
       and rise up to my defense.
3. Wield your spearhead and piercing weapons
          to pierce the hearts and cut through the hatred of those who pursue me.
       Let me hear you say, "I will surely save you."
4. May those who seek to ravage my soul
          be convicted with guilt and shame;
    may those who plot to destroy me
          be ashamed and turn their lives around.
5. Let their plans be empty like husks blown away by the wind,
       dispersed by the angel of the Lord;
6. their methods are dark and slickly presented,
       yet the angel of the Lord runs after them.
7. Because they have laid traps for me without cause
       and without cause sought to trip me up,
8. they will be ruined and never see it coming;
       they entangle themselves in webs of their own deceit,
       they fall to their ruin in the pit they have dug.
9. But I will rejoice in the Lord
       and celebrate his deliverance.
10. With all my being I will proclaim:
       "There is no one like you, O Lord!
    You rescue the humble from the rulers of this selfish world,
       the oppressed and coerced from their abuser."
11. Malicious people make false allegations against me;
       they accuse me of things I know nothing about.
12. They return evil for good
       and it breaks my heart.
13. When they were wounded, my heart ached for them;
       I empathized with fasting, I prayed over and over again from my heart.
14. I was weighed down with concern as for my friends and family.
       I broke down in sorrow, weeping as if it were my mother.

15 But when I was suffering, they got together to laugh;
    they met in secret to plot their attacks—
    they tore me down, constantly slandering me.
16 Full of selfishness, they taunted me without mercy;
    they snarled with hate in their eyes.
17 O Lord, what you've seen—is it enough?
    Bring back my life from their destruction,
    your One and only, from these beastly people.
18 I will glorify you in the great cosmic assembly;
    among the mighty throng I will praise you.
19 Don't let my enemies—all of whom have no reason to be—triumph over me;
    don't let those who hate me without cause
    succeed in their wicked schemes.
20 They do not speak as friends;
    no, they speak words to deceive the peace-lovers on the earth.
21 They open their mouths wide against me and say,
    "Ha! We see how wrong you are."
22 But Lord, you see the truth, so don't remain silent.
    Do not stay away from me, O Lord!
23 Act now and proclaim your verdict;
    fight for me, O Lord my God.
24 Vindicate me, O Lord my God, as your righteousness;
    don't let my enemies gloat over me.
25 Don't let them think, "We did it! We won!"
    Don't let them say, "We have destroyed him."
26 Those who rejoice at my suffering
    will be ashamed and know how wrong they have been;
  those who exalt themselves over me
    will cover themselves in disgrace and humiliation.
27 Those who celebrate my victory of righteousness
    will shout with overwhelming joy and gladness;
  they will never doubt again and they will say forever,
    "Praise be to God who delights in the success of his emissary!"
28 I will tell others of your character and methods of love
    and praise you forevermore. ଔ

PSALM 36

YOUR METHODS ARE SEEN IN THE SKIES

1. Selfishness is cherished deep within the hearts of the wicked;
     they don't admire or respect God
     but are afraid of him because they don't know him.
2. They live in denial, too blinded by pride
     to recognize their own selfish character and to hate its corruption.
3. They lie, blame, distort and speak evil;
     they refuse to behave wisely or with human decency.
4. They lie awake at night, thinking of ways to exploit others;
     everything they do is to advance themselves—
     they never refuse the selfish choice.
5. O Lord, your design-law of love is written in the cosmos,
     the constancy and reliability of your methods are seen in the skies.
6. Your character of love is never-changing, like majestic mountains;
     your discernment penetrates to the deepest sea.
   O Lord, you sustain all life—human and animal alike;
7.   your constant love is the basis of life
     and the only treasure worth possessing!
   All humanity, whether rich or poor,
     find restoration to righteousness only under your care.
8. They will be filled with rich spiritual food from your heavenly home,
     and you will give them drink from the river of life.
9. For you are the fountain of life;
     in your life-giving glory we shine brightly.
10. Perpetually pour your love into those who know and trust you,
     continually pour your righteousness into those
     whose hearts are right with you.
11. Don't let the arrogant and proud walk all over me
     or allow the selfish to bully me.
12. See how the selfish—those who refuse God's design—waste away,
     collapsed and decayed, never to rise again. ೞ

PSALM 37

THE LORD HEALS AND RESTORES

1 Do not be distraught over the apparent gains of the selfish
       or envy those who persist in violating God's design of love;
2 for they will soon wither like grass,
       like flowers of the field they will fade away.
3 Trust in the Lord and live to love others;
       be active in your community as a shepherd of God's kingdom of love.
4 When you delight in the Lord,
       he will give you what your heart desires.
5 Commit yourself to following God's plan—living in harmony with his designs;
       trust him with how life turns out, and he will do what is best:
6 he will renew your character into righteous love that shines brighter every day;
       your decisions will radiate goodness like the noonday sun.
7 Rest in the Lord and be patient for his plan to unfold;
       don't be distraught when the selfish seem to succeed—
       when they carry out their wicked schemes.
8 Don't let anger or resentment take root in your heart;
       don't worry or ruminate—it only inflames selfishness.
9 And selfish people will sever themselves from life,
       but those who trust in the Lord will inherit the earth.
10 It won't be long, and the selfish will be no more;
       you will consider their place in the universe and realize they no longer exist.
11 But the humble who trust the Lord and love others will inherit the earth
       and enjoy everlasting peace.
12 The selfish plot against the unselfish
       and viciously attack them;
13 but the Lord laughs at their foolishness,
       for he sees their end approaching.
14 The selfish draw their knives and load their guns
       to kill the humble and those who refuse to defend themselves—
       to destroy those who live in harmony with God's designs.
15 But their knives cut through their own hearts,
       and their guns will be broken.
16 It is better to be unselfish and poor
       than to be selfish and rich;

17 for the selfish are terminal and will lose all they have,
>   but the unselfish receive life from the Lord.
18 The Lord cares for the unselfish,
>   and they inherit eternal life.
19 In the time of trouble they will not be ashamed;
>   in the days of spiritual famine they will be filled.
20 But the selfish will perish:
>   those who oppose the Lord and his design will be like the fat of rams;
>   consumed in the fires of love, they will go up in smoke.
21 The selfish take from others and do not return,
>   but the unselfish give generously.
22 Those blessed by the Lord will inherit the earth,
>   but those who reject the blessing will be cut off.
23 The Lord heals and restores those
>   who follow his prescription for life;
24 even if they sleep in the grave, they will not be eternally lost,
>   because the Lord holds on to them.
25 Once I was young, but I've lived long and am now old,
>   yet I have never seen the unselfish abandoned by God
>   or their children seeking to feed only themselves.
26 They always give generously and lend freely,
>   and their children live to bless others.
27 Turn from selfishness and love other people—
>   then you will live forever.
28 For the Lord loves the unselfish—those who live right—
>   and will not abandon those who faithfully follow him:
> he watches over them forever,
>   but the children of selfishness will be cut off.
29 The unselfish will inherit the earth
>   and live upon it forever.
30 Those who live in harmony with God's designs speak wisdom,
>   they tell how reality works—what is right and true.
31 God's design protocol (law) is in their heart
>   and they don't sidestep it.
32 The selfish spy on the unselfish,
>   seeking to destroy them;

³³ but the Lord will not abandon them to the power of the selfish
   or let their condemnation stand.
³⁴ Wait expectantly for the Lord
   and live in harmony with his way.
He will regenerate you to inherit the earth;
   you will see: the selfish will be no more.
³⁵ I once saw a selfish and cruel person
   who appeared to grow in influence and power
   like a tree growing in good soil,
³⁶ but when I looked again, they died and were no more:
   though I looked for them, they were nowhere to be found.
³⁷ Take note of the person with mature godly character,
   observe those who live right, for such living results in peace.
³⁸ But all who rebel against God's design will cease to exist;
   the future of the persistently selfish is destruction.
³⁹ The remedy that heals the godly comes from the Lord;
   he is their sanctuary in troubled times.
⁴⁰ The Lord helps them and rescues them;
   he delivers them from the wicked and cures them from their own selfishness
   because they trust in him. ɞ

PSALM 38

YOUR HEALING HAND RESTS UPON ME

¹ O Lord, don't be angry when you discipline me,
   don't be upset when you correct me.
² Your arrows of truth have pierced deep into my heart,
   and your healing hand rests upon me.
³ Because you let me have my way, I am really sick;
   my body is weak and unhealthy because of my sin.
⁴ I am drowning in guilt—
   the weight of it is more than I can bear.
⁵ The initial injury worsens—it festers and rots
   because of my foolish choices.

⁶   I have bent my mind and corrupted my heart;
        I walk in darkness every day—in continual gloom.
⁷   I am filled with shame;
        my body is weak—I feel like I am dying.
⁸   I am burned out and utterly crushed;
        I cry loudly, tormented by the anguish in my heart.
⁹   O Lord, you know what I so desperately long for;
        you hear all my cries.
¹⁰ My heart is pounding; I feel faint,
        and I can hardly see.
¹¹ My friends and neighbors avoid me because of my worsening condition;
        even my family stays away.
¹² And those who want to kill me lay traps for me,
        those who wish me harm talk of my ruin;
        they constantly spread lies about me.
¹³ I am like a deaf person, because their lies don't reach my ears;
        I am like a mute, because I don't speak in my defense;
¹⁴ I am like those who cannot hear
        and whose mouth can offer no reply.
¹⁵ I trust you, O Lord;
        you will be my answer, O Lord my God.
¹⁶ Heal me and don't let my enemies gloat over my distress,
        don't let them boast about my stumbling,
¹⁷ for I am about to collapse—
        my heart is in constant pain.
¹⁸ I confess the selfishness within me;
        I so desperately want to be cured!
¹⁹ I have many zealous enemies
        who hate me without reason.
²⁰ They repay evil for good;
        they slander the good I do, determined to make it appear evil.
²¹ O Lord, don't leave me;
        stay close to me, O my God.
²² Quickly, help me now,
        O Lord my Healer. ⋘

PSALM 39

I PUT MY HOPE IN YOU!

1   I have decided, "I will be careful how I live
        and will not sin by what I say;
        I will guard my speech while around evil people who will twist my words."

2   But as I stood there in silence, not saying a word—
        not even anything good—my frustration only increased.

3   My heart flamed with irritation,
        and as I thought about it, I grew more impatient, so I spoke these words:

4   "Reveal to me the end of my life—how it turns out—
        the measure of my character;
        help me to understand how little time I have.

5   You have given me life for just a short time;
        my lifespan is like a moment to you.
        Even the oldest human life is like a vapor—it quickly passes away.

6   The truth is: Every human is a dead-person walking—
        a mere shadow fading away;
    all their selfish work is for nothing.
        They hoard wealth, but who will spend it when they are gone?

7   So where do I put my hope, Lord?
        I put my hope in you!

8   Heal me from all my deviations from your design;
        do not leave me to fade away in disgrace.

9   I am speechless; I have nothing to say for myself,
        for you have convinced me.

10 You can stop holding my feet to the fire;
        my denial is over and I'm ready to die to selfishness.

11 You confront and discipline people for their deviations from your designs for life;
        their self-sufficiency you consume like a dry grass—
        every human is but a vapor.

12 Hear my request, O Lord, listen to my cry for help;
        comfort me when I weep.
    For I am just passing through this world, completely dependent on you,
        a stranger here, just like my ancestors were.

13 Remove your discipline from me, that I may rejoice once again
        before I depart and am no more." ໒

Psalm 40
Many are the Marvelous Wonders You Have Done

1 With eager expectation I looked for the Lord:
    he drew near to me and heard me crying.
2 I was drowning in despair, near death, but he pulled me out;
    he pulled me out of the miry abyss.
  He placed me on the solid Rock
    and gave me a new firm standing.
3 He inspired me to sing a new song—
    praise to our God of love.
  May many see what God has done and be overwhelmed with admiration
    and trust the Lord completely.
4 Happy are the people
    who trust the Lord unreservedly,
  who do not turn to the self-sufficient—
    to those who promote the false gods who can be moved by bloody sacrifice.
5 Many, O Lord my God,
    are the marvelous wonders you have done,
  your magnificent design for life and plan for us—
    no one could describe them all.
  I will proclaim and speak of them,
    yet there are more than I could ever tell.
6 You never desired sacrifices or offerings,
    but an open heart eager to understand.
  Burnt offerings and sin offerings
    are not what your heart longed for.
7 Then I said, "Here I am, I have come—
    I am the One written about in the Scriptures.
8 I have come to fulfill your will of love, O my God;
    your character, methods and design of love are within my heart."
9 Before the entire universe I have proved your method of love to be right;
    I always speak the truth,
    as you, O Lord, already know.
10 I have not kept to myself your plan to heal and restore humanity;
    I tell of your constancy—that your design-laws never change—
    and of your remedy.

I have revealed to the entire universe
  your methods of love and truth.
¹¹ O Lord, you do not withhold your compassionate mercy from me;
  your love and truth always protect me.
¹² For numerous evils swarm all around me;
  the corruption to your design has taken hold on me,
  and I cannot see through it.
The breaks to your design are more than the hairs on my head,
  and my heart fails within me.
¹³ Be pleased and deliver me, O Lord;
  hurry, Lord, help me now!
¹⁴ Let those who seek to kill me
  experience shame and humiliation;
let all who seek to harm me
  run away in guilt and disgrace.
¹⁵ Let those who mocked and jeered at me
  be destroyed by their own shame.
¹⁶ But may everyone who seeks you
  be restored to health and happiness as they unite with you;
may those who love your remedy always say,
  "The Lord is the greatest!"
¹⁷ As for me, I have no strength and I need you,
  so keep me in your thoughts, O Lord.
You are my helper and my healer;
  O my God, act quickly! ∝

Psalm 41

He will provide remedy to our sin-sickness

1   Happy and spiritually-healthy are those who care for the helpless;
     in the time of trouble the Lord will deliver them.

2   The Lord will preserve their individuality and give them eternal life;
     they will live and be happy upon the earth.
     The Lord will not give them up to die from selfishness—their enemy.

3   He will provide remedy to their sin-sickness
     and restore them back to his perfect design.

4   I said, "O Lord, pour your grace upon me;
     heal and restore me, for I have gone against your design for life."

5   My enemies voice their selfish hate toward me:
     they say, "When will he finally die and be forgotten?"

6   When one of them comes to visit me,
     they pretend to be my friend
    but secretly seek something to twist and misrepresent,
     then they go out and spread their false accusations abroad.

7   All who hate me connive together, whispering their lies about me;
     they construe things about me in the worst way possible.

8   They say, "He is putrid with sin and selfishness;
     he will not rise again from where he lies."

9   Even my close and trusted friend who shares my bread
     lifts up his heel against me.

10   But you, O Lord, pour your life-giving power upon me;
     raise me up, that I may be perfectly whole to offer them remedy.

11   I know that you are pleased with me,
     because my enemy—death—has not triumphed over me.

12   You accept and receive me because I am blameless;
     you establish me in your presence forever.

13   Thanksgiving and adoration to the Creator, the God of those who prevail,
     from everlasting to everlasting—
     so let it always be! ∞

PSALM 42

THE LORD CONSTANTLY LOVES ME

1   As the deer longs for the refreshing streams,
      so my heart longs for you, O God.
2   My entire being thirsts for God—the life-giving God.
      When will I be restored to live in his presence?
3   Day and night
      I cry so hard I cannot eat;
   all the while my enemies taunt me,
      "Where is your God?"
4   These are things I remember
      as my life drains away:
   on account of the multitude,
      I went to the house of God
   with rejoicing and thanksgiving
      and the sound of great celebration.
5   Then why is my heart breaking?
      Why is the pain so overwhelming?
   But I will put my hope in God,
      and I will yet praise him—my Deliverer and my God.
6   Yet, my heart is breaking with overwhelming grief;
      so I will remember your goodness and trustworthiness
   while suffering—in the region of the Jordan,
      in the region of Mount Hermon, and from the small hill.
7   Deep waves of grief call forth deeper waves of sorrow
      washing over me in a crushing roar;
   surging waves of heartache and drowning tides of despair
      sweep over me.
8   The Lord constantly loves me,
      and his song is within my heart:
      an ode to the Creator God—the source of life.
9   I say to God, my foundation for life,
      "How long will you hold back?
   How long will the darkness last—
      the oppression of the enemy?"

¹⁰ The rejection and taunts of my enemies
>> pierce me to the bone.
> They constantly mock me, saying,
>> "Where is your God?"
¹¹ Why is my heart breaking?
>> Why is the pain so overwhelming?
> I will put my hope in God,
>> and I will yet praise him—
>> my Deliverer and my God. ❧

PSALM 43

O GOD, YOU ARE MY STRENGTH

¹ O God, disclose my spiritual health for all to see:
>> prove my harmony with your design,
> defend me from the legal condemnation of the ungodly world,
>> deliver me from the deceitful human system.
² O God, you are my strength.
>> For how long will you let me go?
> How long must I endure this grief—
>> the oppression of the enemy?
³ Release your fire of truth
>> to lead and guide me,
> and bring me into your sanctuary,
>> that I may live with you in your home.
⁴ Then I will go to the place of God's sacrifice
>> and join together with God in heartfelt joy and celebration.
> I will praise and thank you with the harp,
>> O God, my mighty God.
⁵ How long must my heart despair?
>> How long will the torment last?
> Wait for the Lord!
>> For I will again praise him—
>> my Healer and my God. ❧

PSALM 44

YOU ARE MY KING AND MY GOD

1   We have heard the stories with our own ears, O God,
    for our ancestors have told us
    of the amazing feats you performed in their days—in days long ago:

2   how by your therapeutic intervention
    you removed the nations that were beyond healing
    and established our ancestors as your helpers;
how you cut off the necrotic nations
    and nurtured our ancestors.

3   Your helpers didn't take the land by their weapons—
    it wasn't their strong army that gave them victory:
it was your power and your will,
    and the fires of truth and love shining from you,
    for you fulfilled your pleasure through them.

4   You are my King and my God;
    provide for the healing of those who prevail in union with you.

5   Only by your power of truth and love
    can we push back our selfish and hateful enemies;
    only by your character of love can we rise above our foes.

6   I have no faith in guns,
    and knives will not heal me;

7   but you heal our hearts from the attacks of the enemy—
    those without love, who are consumed by shame.

8   O God, we always give you the credit
    and will praise your character and methods of love forever.

9   You have rejected our self-sufficiency and you humbled us;
    we marched to war in our own strength, and you let us go.

10 We return to you from the enemy—
    from the selfish and hateful who seek to exploit us.

11 You let us go, but we were like sheep ready to be slaughtered
    and have been scattered among the nations.

12 We sold ourselves for nothing
    and gained nothing from the sale.

¹³ We disgraced ourselves to our neighbors,
and they mock, ridicule and scorn us.
¹⁴ We have made ourselves a joke to the nations;
people shake their heads in disgust.
¹⁵ I can't escape the constant humiliation;
shame is written all over my face.
¹⁶ All I hear are the taunts and mocking from those who hate me—
those enemies bent on revenge.
¹⁷ All this happened to us
even though not all of us rejected or betrayed you.
¹⁸ Not all of us have been disloyal to you;
not all of us have walked away from your plan.
¹⁹ But you allowed the dragon to crush us
and the shadow of death to wash over us.
²⁰ If we had rejected the character and methods of our Creator God
and given our loyalty and devotion to a false god,
²¹ you would know it,
since you know the hidden secrets of the heart.
²² It is for the outworking of your healing plan that we face death every day;
we are treated as sheep led to the slaughter.
²³ Rise up, O Lord! How long will you wait to act?
Take action! Do not leave us to our own way forever!
²⁴ Why do you wait?
Why do you leave us in our misery and suffering?
²⁵ We can't do it on our own—we humble ourselves in the dust;
we are worn out, with faces in the dirt.
²⁶ Rise up and help us;
heal us because of your unfailing love. ଔ

Psalm 45

The foundation of your government will last forever

1   My heart is filled with a beautiful truth
        as I recite my sonnet for the king;
        my tongue is like the pen of an accomplished writer.
2   You are the most perfect son of man;
        grace pours forth from your mouth,
        because God has blessed you forever.
3   Take up your sword of truth, O Mighty One;
        reveal your glorious and majestic character of love.
4   In your perfect character of love, ride forth victoriously.
        In truth, in humble condescension and harmony with God's design,
        let your life reveal your awesome achievements.
5   May your sharp arrows of truth pierce the hearts of king's enemies,
        and may the nations fall prostrate before you.
6   The foundation of your government—the throne of your authority—O God,
        will last forever, and righteousness will be the governing principle.
7   You have loved the methods of righteousness—
        the methods of love, truth and freedom—
    and hated the way of wickedness
        with its principles of selfishness, deceit and coercion,
    therefore God, your God, has set you above all beings
        by anointing you with the oil of joy.
8   You are dressed in the most beautiful character,
        sweet like the most fragrant myrrh, aloes and cinnamon;
        from within the heavenly temple you rejoice.
9   Daughters of world-rulers are your honored guests,
        and your bride stands beside you, dressed in the gold of a godly character.
10 Bride of the king, listen to what I say:
        Forget the place of your birth and your father's estate,
11 for the king greatly desires to make you beautiful;
        worship him, for he is the Lord.
12 The children of this selfish world will come with their gifts;
        people of wealth will seek your affection.
13 The bride is absolutely glorious—
        adorned in the gold of a Godlike character.

14 Dressed in beautifully embroidered clothing, she is led to the king;
  her loyal and pure-hearted friends go with her.
15 They come overflowing with joy and gladness
  and enter the king's palace.
16 Your children will replace those from the ancient past;
  you will make them rulers over the entire earth.
17 I will cause your character of love to be remembered through all generations—
  then the nations will praise you for ever and ever. ଔ

PSALM 46
THE CREATOR GOD IS WITH US

1 In union with God we are safe and strong;
  he is always present and ready to help when we are in trouble.
2 Therefore, we won't be afraid even if the earth's ecosystem fails
  and the mountains collapse into the sea,
3 and the oceans rage with devastating storms
  and the hills shake at their roaring fury.
4 There is a river whose streams bring health and happiness to the city of God—
  that holy place where the Most High dwells.
5 God abides in that city—it will not be destroyed;
  God will save her when the morning comes.
6 Nations are raging and kingdoms crumble;
  God's voice thunders, and the earth melts into molten rock.
7 The Creator God is with us;
  the God whom Jacob trusted is our protection.
8 Come and see the works of the Lord—
  the demolition of all defects to his design on the earth.
9 He ends all wars, division and conflict throughout the entire earth;
  he destroys guns and demolishes all weapons of war,
  he burns through human defenses with the fires of love and truth.
10 "Stop striving to save yourselves, and know that I am God—your Creator;
  I will heal the people, I will restore the earth."
11 The Lord Almighty is with us;
  the God whom Jacob trusted is our protector. ଔ

PSALM 47

GOD REIGNS ENTHRONED IN HIS HOLY PERFECTION

1 Come, everyone—all people of the earth—clap your hands,
   cheer for the Lord, celebrate him with shouts of joy!
2 For the Lord God, the Almighty Creator, is overwhelming and awesome—
   the great King who governs the entire earth!
3 He speaks to all the nations among us,
   to the people placed at our feet.
4 He has chosen the earth as our home—
   the radiant possession of those, who with God, prevail.
5 In our hearts, God has risen with shouts of joy;
   we adore the Lord with the praise of trumpets.
6 Sing praise to God, sing praises;
   sing praise to our King—sing praises!
7 For God is the Creator and Ruler of all the earth;
   sing to him your heartfelt praise.
8 God rules over the entire world;
   God reigns enthroned in his holy perfection.
9 The leaders of the nations gather before him,
   as do the people of the God whom Abraham trusted,
   for the laws of nature that life is built upon belong to God—
   the God who reigns supreme. ❧

PSALM 48

THE SUPREME LORD WILL BE GLORIFIED

1 The supreme Lord will be glorified
   in the city of our God, his dwelling place.
2 Beautiful to look upon,
   the center of universal joy
   is Zion—that holy hill—
   the city of God, the Great King.
3 God has revealed
   that he is the safety

for those who live in that city.

4 The rulers of this selfish world unite together
and move to attack the great city,

5 but when they see the truth shine forth,
they are shocked and run away in terror.

6 They shake with fear and anguish,
crying out in pain like a woman in labor.

7 The Spirit of truth crushes them
like a strong east wind shatters the largest ships.

8 We have heard of God's mighty deeds,
and now we have seen them
in the city of the Lord of the stars—the God of all creation—
the city of our God,
built by him to last forever.

9 Fitted for the interior of your Temple,
we reflect your perfect, never-failing love, O God.

10 Your character of love, our dear God,
is praised in every world throughout the universe;
you always use your power to heal, restore and do what is right.

11 The New Jerusalem rejoices,
the towns filled with the victorious are happy and healthy,
because what you have decided is right.

12 Examine the New Jerusalem thoroughly, walk about her,
and take note how she rises;

13 mark in your heart the pain of her birth
and view her palaces,
that you may tell of it for all eternity.

14 For this God is our God for ever and ever;
he will lead us until the end of time. ❦

Psalm 49

No human can buy the remedy from God

1 Hear this, everyone;
　　listen carefully, every person who lives on the earth,
2 both young and old,
　　rich and poor alike:
3 I will tell you real wisdom,
　　because I understand how reality works.
4 I will use my insight to discern profound proverbs
　　and bring forth the hidden meaning, like music from a harp.
5 Why should I fear in the days when evil abounds,
　　when the depravity and villainy of my enemies surround me—
6 those who believe they are spiritually superior because of their wealth
　　and boast of their great riches?
7 No one can ever cure their own terminal condition,
　　no human can buy the remedy from God—
8 the cost to procure it is beyond our means.
　　Nothing we could provide would ever cure our mortal state
9 so that we would live forever
　　and never experience death.
10 For all can see that everyone dies—
　　the wise, the foolish and the thoughtless brutes—
　　everyone perishes and leaves their wealth to others.
11 Their inner thoughts (characters) are fixed
　　as their permanent state of being.
　　Though they claimed the earth as their own,
12 their prized selfish—sin-infected—world will not last:
　　they will die just like brute beasts.
13 This is the inevitable end for those who trust in themselves,
　　and of all who follow them and embrace their selfish ways.
14 Like mindless sheep they are destined for the grave,
　　and death will consume them.
　　When the earth is made new,
　　the righteous—those restored to God's perfect design—
　　will walk over their graves;
　　their bodies will turn to dust in the grave,

and they will never live in heavenly mansions.
¹⁵ But God will heal my terminal condition and resurrect me from the grave;
    he will most certainly take me to live with him.
¹⁶ Don't be distraught when the selfish become rich,
    when their estates become increasingly opulent and grand,
¹⁷ for they will take nothing with them when they die—
    their wealth will not follow them into the grave.
¹⁸ Though they proclaim themselves fulfilled and triumphant—
    and they are praised for their success—
¹⁹ they will die like all the other selfish people before them;
    they will never see the light of life again.
²⁰ A person who is wealthy without understanding the reality of God's design
    is like the mindless beast doomed to perish. ❧

PSALM 50

"I WILL HEAL YOU"

¹ The Mighty God, Creator of heaven and earth speaks;
    he calls to the whole earth from one horizon to the other.
² From heaven—perfect and beautiful—
    God shines forth.
³ Our Creator God is coming and will not ignore the defects to his design;
    a fire of truth and love consumes all corruption and death;
    all around him is whirlwind of re-creative energy.
⁴ He calls on the heavenly beings above and humans on earth below
    to witness how he deals with his people:
⁵ "Gather to me those who have partaken of my remedy—
    those who have agreed to follow my treatment plan
    and have sacrificed self to do so."
⁶ The heavenly beings make know that God is right,
    for God himself is judged to be right.
⁷ "Listen, my people, to what I say;
    listen, you who with me prevail, and I will testify among you:
    I am God, your Creator.
⁸ I do not correct you for carrying out the symbolic sacrifices,

though you continually bring me your ceremonial offerings.
9 But understand that I have no need of your bulls
    or the goats from your pens,
10 for every animal in the forest is already mine,
    and the cattle on thousands of hills.
11 I know every bird that flies in the air,
    and the insects of the field are mine.
12 I would not tell you if I were hungry,
    for the entire world and everything in it is mine.
13 I don't eat the flesh of bulls
    or drink the blood of goats.
14 So bring me what matters—a heart thankful to God,
    and give the Most High your loyalty, just as you have promised;
15 call upon me when you are hurting and distressed,
    and I will heal you, transforming your character,
    and you will glorify me."
16 But to the persistently selfish, God says:
    "O how you talk about my commandments
    and claim to be in agreement with me,
17 but you hate my methods
    and ignore what I say.
18 When you see the snatcher of souls, you unite with him;
    you join with adulterers—those who break their vows.
19 You speak evil continually
    and never hesitate to lie.
20 You find fault with your own family
    and slander your own relatives.
21 All these things you have done and I have quietly let you,
    so you thought I was exactly like you.
    But I will correct you;
    you will face the truth of your own corrupt condition.
22 Think carefully, you who have rejected the truth about God,
    lest you be torn apart with no one left to save you.
23 Those with thankful hearts glorify me;
    those who follow my plan I will surely heal. ❧

PSALM 51

CREATE IN ME A SELFLESS AND PURE HEART, O GOD

1   Be merciful to me, O God,
       because you are unfailing love.
    Because you are compassionate,
       eradicate my sinfulness.
2   Cleanse me from all deviations from your design
       and wash away all my selfishness.
3   For I know how horrible is my departure from your love,
       and thoughts of my selfish acts constantly oppress me.
4   Against you—above all others—have I sinned,
       I have chosen what is evil in your eyes;
    so that you are proved right and true in what you say
       and proved to be right when you are judged.
5   Behold the reality of the situation: I was selfish when I was born—
       selfish from the moment my mother conceived me.
6   Behold another reality: You will restore love and honesty into my inmost self;
       you will write your wisdom into my heart.
7   Purge my heart with your remedy and I will be renewed;
       wash me and I will be whiter than snow.
8   Restore to me joy and gladness;
       remove the crushing guilt and shame from me.
9   Please don't look at the mess I have made
       but erase all my selfishness from within me.
10 Create in me a selfless and pure heart, O God,
       and put a new and loyal mind within me.
11 Don't banish me from your presence
       or take your Holy Spirit from me.
12 Restore to me the joy of your healing and restoration
       and grant me a willing mind to comply with your treatment plan.
13 Then I will teach your healing ways to those out of harmony with your design,
       and the selfish will turn to you.
14 Remove from me the heart of a murderer, O God—
       my Creator who transforms me—
       and I will sing of your righteousness.

¹⁵ O Lord, inspire the words of my mouth
and I will proclaim the beauty of your character.
¹⁶ You do not desire animal sacrifice, or I would bring it;
you do not want ritual offerings.
¹⁷ The sacrifice you desire is a humble and teachable attitude;
a broken and repentant heart you will not reject, O God.
¹⁸ Because the people of Zion are your helpers,
enable them to spread the truth, and strengthen the defenses of Jerusalem.
¹⁹ Then the animal sacrifices will become effective teaching tools
and ritual offerings that enlightened minds will please you;
then bulls will again be properly offered on your altar. ⟡

PSALM 52

I TRUST IN GOD'S UNFAILING LOVE

1 How you boast, O mighty one,
    of the evil you originated!
    But God's unfailing love is eternal.
2 You plot ways to destroy;
    your tongue is razor-sharp, cutting at the truth with your lies,
    you father of lies.
3 You love evil—inflicting pain and causing suffering—rather than doing good;
    you misrepresent, deceive and distort rather than saying what is right.
4 You love every word that injures or destroys,
    you lying snake!
5 It is certain that God will break your power and overthrow you forever:
    He will pull you out and remove
every trace of your selfish and deceitful ways
    from human hearts and minds where you have dwelt;
    you will be permanently exterminated—removed from the land of the living.
6 Those restored to God's design will see and be in awe of God;
    they will see the evil one and laugh with relief, saying:
7 "Here is the one who rejected God
    and left the safety of God's kingdom,
who trusted in the abundance of his own abilities
    and grew in power by destroying others!"
8 But I am like a flourishing olive tree
    firmly rooted in the family of God;
I trust in God's unfailing love
    for ever and ever.
9 For all eternity I will thank you, God, for what you have done;
    I will rely on your character of love,
    for all holy beings now know that you are good. ෆ

Psalm 53

I long for the remedy which heals God's people

1. Fools comfort themselves by saying,
       "There is no God."
   They are corrupt with selfishness and do disgusting things;
       there is not one who lives in harmony with God's design of love.
2. God looks down from heaven
       on the entire human race
   to see if there is anyone who understands his design for life—
       anyone who seeks a saving relationship with God.
3. The entire human race has accepted lies about God
       and turned away from him.
   They have become completely necrotic in character;
       there is no one who does good—
   who loves others, who is selfless and kind—
       not even one.
4. Will the selfish exploiters of others never learn—
       those who suck the life out of others like gluttons devour bread
       and who refuse to talk to God?
5. One day they will be overwhelmed with terror—
       terrified like they have never before known.
   God will annihilate the enemies of the righteous;
       they will be shamed before you, for God has rejected them.
6. I long for the remedy, which heals God's people, to come out of heaven!
       When God restores his people,
       those who prevail with him will be glad! ཙ

PSALM 54

GOD IS HERE AND HE IS MY HELPER

1   Heal me, O God, by your character of love;
     defend me by your power.

2   Listen to me, O God;
     take special note of what I say.

3   Villains are attacking me;
     cruel people are trying to kill me—selfish people who care nothing for God.

4   But look! God is here and he is my helper;
     the Lord is the One who sustains my life.

5   Those who plot evil for me will reap the evil they have sown;
     the truth is that they will be cut off from life.

6   I freely sacrifice myself for you;
     I will reveal your character of love, O Lord, for it is good.

7   For you have set me free from all that enslaved me,
     and I now understand my true enemy. ❧

PSALM 55

GOD HAS RULED IN LOVE FOR ALL ETERNITY

1   As I talk to you, O God, take seriously what I say
        and consider earnestly my plea;
2   take to heart what I am saying and give me your best answer.
        I am restless, uneasy; with my mind unable to relax,
        I am in agony of thought
3   because the words of the enemies echo in my head.
        The selfish glare at me
    and seek to bring evil down upon me;
        they hate me and are bitter toward me.
4   My heart is pounding in my chest;
        I am terrified—I feel like I am going to die.
5   Panic-stricken, I shake uncontrollably;
        I feel like I am drowning—it is horrible!
6   I cry, "Oh, if I only had wings like a dove!
        I could escape; I could fly away and be safe—
7   I would fly far away
        and rest in a quiet place free of people;
8   I would swoop down quickly to my safe haven,
        far from the blowhards and the rages and tempests of life."
9   Destroy their wicked words and silence their speech,
        for I have seen violence and fighting inhabit their city.
10   Day and night hostility prowls its walls;
        selfishness, hatred and abuse live within it.
11   Destruction is everywhere;
        fraud and extortion are rampant in its streets.
12   If it was only an enemy that was insulting me,
        I could handle it;
    if it was only someone who hated me that was against me,
        I could avoid them;
13   but it is you—my counselors,
        my confidants, my dear friends!
14   We had such a good friendship, sharing our hearts with each other;
        we even worshipped together in God's temple.

¹⁵ Desolation swirls round about them;
>> may death take them quickly,
>> for evil and selfishness are permanent residents in their hearts.
¹⁶ But I will call to God for help,
>> and the Lord will heal me.
¹⁷ No matter when it is—morning, noon or night—that I voice my concerns,
>> he hears me.
¹⁸ He restores my inner self to his perfect design,
>> healing all the damage from the war
>> despite all those who opposed me.
¹⁹ God, who has ruled in love for all eternity,
>> will proclaim their accurate diagnosis
>> that they are hardened in selfishness beyond change—
>> they have no respect for God.
²⁰ My former friends attack those with whom they have agreements;
>> they betray their trust.
²¹ They speak smooth words to butter a person up,
>> but in their hearts, they plot their attack;
>> their words are like oil, intended to soften a person up
>> as they seek to stab them in the back.
²² Pour all your worries, frustrations and burdens on the Lord
>> and he will care for you;
>> he never allows those restored to his design to be lost.
²³ But you, O God, will not prevent the wicked from going down
>> into decay in the grave—murderers and liars will die young.
>> But as for me, I trust in you. ❧

Psalm 56

I Glory in God, Standing Confidently Upon the Truth

1 Show your favor for me, O God, for people walk all over me;
    they constantly oppress me—they won't let up.

2 Every day my adversaries trample on me;
    the many who attack me think they are better than me.

3 When I am afraid,
    I will trust in you.

4 I glory in God, standing confidently upon the truth;
    I trust completely in God and his methods of love—I will not live in fear:
    what can mere mortals do to me?

5 They constantly misrepresent what I say;
    they use all their abilities to plot ways to harm me.

6 They slither in the shadows, conspiring together;
    they watch every step I take,
    craving an opportunity to destroy me.

7 The pain and sorrow caused by deviating from your design
    they cannot escape;
    indeed, how low have the people fallen, O God!

8 You have recorded my grief;
    you have taken away my tears—
    is not my character transcribed in your book?

9 My enemies will turn their backs when I proclaim the truth,
    but this I know: God is for me.

10 I glory in God, standing confidently upon the truth.
    I glory in the Lord, standing confidently upon the truth;

11 I trust completely in God and his methods of love—
    I will not live in fear:
    what can mere mortals do to me?

12 As I have vowed to you, O God,
    I give my life an offering of thanksgiving to you.

13 For you have saved me from death;
    you have kept me from stepping out of harmony with your design for life,
that I may walk in God's presence—
    in the light of his life-giving glory. ❧

PSALM 57

YOUR GREAT LOVE IS THE BASIS OF LIFE IN THE UNIVERSE

1   Show your favor to me, O God, show your favor to me,
        for I have surrendered my life into your care.
     In the shade beneath your wings I am safe and secure
        until the storms of life have passed.
2   I call out to God—Ruler of heaven and earth,
        the Creator—who completes his work in me.
3   He sends his Remedy from heaven and heals me,
        saving me from the guilt and condemnation
     that seek to consume me;
        God sends his never-failing love and liberating truth.
4   Enemies, like lions, surround me;
        I sleep among people who are like ravenous beasts—
     seeking to devour others—
     whose biting and sharp comments pierce hearts like arrows,
        whose words cut deeply like swords.
5   Rise up and take action from heaven, O God;
        let your glory shine over the entire earth.
6   My enemies have set a trap for me,
        and I am tired and worn down.
     They dug a pit in my path,
        but they have fallen into it themselves.
7   My mind is set, O God,
        my heart is settled;
        I will sing your praises.
8   I will awake!
        The harp and lyre will come alive!
        I will awaken in the morning.
9   I will give thanks to you, O Lord, among the people;
        I will sing your praise with the family of God.
10   For your great love is the basis of life in the entire universe,
        and your truth—the foundation of the smallest particle of matter.
11   Rise up and take action from heaven, O God;
        let your glory shine over the entire earth. ೞ

PSALM 58

TRULY, THERE IS A GOD OF LOVE

1. Do you speak what is right, or remain silent?
   Do you govern the people fairly—do what is good for others?
2. No! Your hearts are selfish and you plot to advantage yourselves;
   you orchestrate violent crimes throughout the earth.
3. Their whole life long, the wicked refuse healing;
   from birth they persist in selfishness, lies and breaking God's design.
4. Their ways are poisonous like the venom of a snake;
   they are unresponsive to truth, like a deaf cobra
5. that doesn't respond to the music of the snake charmer,
   no matter how masterfully the charmer plays.
6. Pull out their fangs, O God;
   muzzle the mouth of those ravenous brutes, O Lord!
7. They fade away like water soaking into dry ground;
   they wither away like grass.
8. They are like a snail that melts into slime,
   like a stillborn fetus that never sees the light.
9. These unclean vessels don't learn from their thorny and destructive choices—
   whether young or old—
   the persistently selfish will be angry when they are all swept away.
10. The healed—those with Godlike hearts—
    will be glad when selfishness is eradicated;
    they will wash from their lives the blood, pain and loss caused by the wicked.
11. Then people will say,
    "There truly is a reward for those who are Godlike in heart;
    truly, there is a God of love who rules the entire earth." ☙

76

Psalm 59

You are my refuge, my God of perfect love

1 Save me from my enemies, O my God;
    protect from those who rise up against me.

2 Save me from the selfish—those who exploit others—
    and from murderers.

3 Look how they lurk in the shadows, seeking to take my life!
    The strong and mighty in this selfish world conspire against me,
    but not because I offended or did something wrong, O Lord.

4 Though I have done nothing wrong, they are determined to attack me—
    come, stand beside me and see.

5 O Majestic God, Creator and God of all who in union with you prevail,
    step in and take charge of the persistently selfish who oppose your remedy;
    don't reward or show favor to the liars, cheats and backstabbers.

6 They come out when the sun goes down;
    howling like dogs, they prowl about the city.

7 They vomit filth from their mouths—
    their words are like daggers flying forth to pierce and wound, so why listen?

8 You, O Lord, don't take their words seriously;
    you know their words are evidence of their corruption.

9 You are my strength, so I will cling to you;
    you, O God, are my refuge.

10 The God of love will come to me,
    he will help me see who my enemies are.

11 Don't kill them,
    for the people will quickly forget and continue to ignore you.
  Instead, use your power to shake their self-sufficient world,
    bring them down from their haughtiness.

12 Because they misrepresent your design
    and promote a false remedy,
    they are imprisoned by their own pride.
  Because they are sworn to the lies they speak,

13 their poisonous beliefs will destroy them—
    destroy them completely.
  Then all will understand how God rules—as revealed in Israel

and shown throughout the entire world.

14 They come out when the sun goes down;
       howling like dogs, they prowl about the city.

15 They roam around looking for something to devour
       and howl when nothing satisfies.

16 But I will sing of your strength;
       I will sing of your never-failing love in the morning,
    for you are my safe haven—
       my healing sanctuary in the time of trouble.

17 I will sing of God my strength;
       you, O God, are my refuge, my God of perfect love. ℘

Psalm 60

In union with God, we will be restored

1 O God, you have let us go our own way, and we are broken down;
   you have been displeased with our selfishness—
   please come back and restore us!

2 The nation is fractured and split apart;
   heal its wounds, for we are shaken and about to fall.

3 You have let us see how hard life is when we leave you:
   you let us drink the wine of our own ideas
   and we no longer walk the straight and narrow way.

4 But for those who revere you and love your ways,
   you have given a standard
   that they may follow to avoid destruction.

5 Heal and restore us with your power,
   that those who accept your love may be transformed.

6 God has spoken from his dwelling place:
   "I will rejoice to give humanity the earth—
   all of it, until east meets west.

7 Gilead in the east and Manasseh in the west are mine;
   Ephraim will be a strong leader,
   Judah will be the father of the Sovereign.

8 Enemies like Moab will be washed away,
   foes like Edom will be cast off like a worn-out shoe.
   Because of me, enemies like Philistia cry out."

9 Who will lead me into the fortified city?
   Who will lead me into Edom?

10 O God, you haven't given up on us, have you?
   Is it you refusing to fight in our behalf?

11 O help us out of our affliction,
   for all our efforts to save ourselves are worthless.

12 In union with God, we will be restored—strong and healthy,
   and he will defeat our enemy. ⚓

PSALM 61

LEAD ME BACK TO YOU, MY ROCK WHO LIFTS ME UP

1.   O God, listen closely to my plea;
        pay special attention to my prayer.
2.   From the ends of the earth I call out to you—
        overwhelmed, discouraged, and feeling like I cannot go on—
        lead me back to you, my Rock who lifts me up.
3.   For you have always been my refuge—
        an impenetrable fortress—from the enemy.
4.   I will live in your sanctuary forever:
        safe in your presence, covered in your glory.
5.   For you have heard my commitment to you, O God,
        and you have given me the reward due to those
        who revere your character of love.
6.   Give the king a long life,
        spanning several generations.
7.   May he live in God's presence forever,
        preserved by your never-failing love and truth.
8.   Then my life will be a perpetual song of praise to your character of love—
        a fulfillment of my commitment to you every day of my life. ∞

Psalm 62

My inmost-self finds rest only in God

1   My inmost-self finds rest only in God;
        my healing and restoration come from him.
2   He alone defends and heals me;
        he is my remedy, so I will not be destroyed.
3   How long will all of you verbally attack me?
        Will you go beyond words and try to kill me—
        to knock me over like a tottering fence or leaning wall?
4   Your goal is to tear me down,
        to knock me off my place of esteem; you love to lie.
    You speak friendly words to my face
        but curse me in your hearts.
5   My inmost-self finds rest only in God;
        my confidence comes from him.
6   He alone defends and heals me;
        he is my remedy, so I will not be destroyed.
7   God recreates and exalts me;
        He is my strong foundation, my safe harbor.
8   O people, trust God always
        and pour out your hearts to him,
        for God is our safe haven.
9   Children of selfishness are only an expiring breath;
        selfish people are untrustworthy liars.
    When weighed on the scales of life, they have no health;
        they have nothing beneficial to offer.
10 Do not seek security in extortion;
        do not hope to excel by robbery.
    If you do become rich,
        do not place your heart's peace in your wealth.
11 One thing God has spoken plainly
        (and I have heard it many times),
    that all life, health and strength come from God,
12   and that God is love.
    Every person will receive from God
        what they have chosen for themselves. ∽

Psalm 63

I HAVE SEEN YOU IN YOUR HOLINESS

1   O God, my Creator God,
     I long for you;
  my inmost-self thirsts for your love—the water of life;
     my body aches for your healing touch
  in this selfish world, parched and dying—
     a world without your living water.

2   Yes, I have seen you in your holiness;
     I dwell upon your strength and your glorious character of love.

3   Because your love is the basis, goodness and beauty of life,
     I will praise you.

4   I will glorify you with my entire life,
     and with a character renewed—to be just like you—I will talk with you.

5   My inmost-self is fully nourished with your bountiful feast;
     I will sing songs of praise and thanksgiving to you.

6   As I lay in bed, I will remember you;
     throughout the night I will think of you.

7   You have always been there to help me;
     I rejoice under your protective care.

8   I cling tightly to you,
     and you hold me safe in your powerful right hand.

9   But those who seek to destroy my life
     will destroy themselves and disintegrate into the soil of the earth.

10   They are released to their kill-or-be-killed methods
     and will be consumed by wild animals.

11   But the king will rejoice in God;
     all who agree with God, receiving his character,
     will live and praise him,
  but all who prefer lies will cease to exist—
     their mouths will be eternally silenced. ∝

PSALM 64

LET ALL THOSE WITH HEARTS SET RIGHT WITH GOD PRAISE HIM!

1   My dearest God, listen as I pour out my heartache to you:
    Deliver me from fear—the fear of the enemy;
2   conceal me from the schemes of the selfish—
    from the loveless mob of evildoers.
3   Their tongues are sharp—cutting like swords;
    their words are piercing like deadly arrows.
4   They tear down good people without warning;
    they attack mercilessly and without remorse.
5   They spur each other on into greater selfishness,
    they plan how to cover their tracks and hide their traps;
    they say, "No one will catch us."
6   They plot wickedness and say,
    "We have devised the perfect crime!
    None can read our minds—our schemes are secret."
7   But God will shoot them with his arrows of truth,
    and suddenly they will be struck with guilt and fear.
8   He will use their own words to diagnose them accurately—
    their own selfish characters will ruin them;
    all who see them as they truly are will mourn.
9   Then all humanity will be in awe;
    they will tell what God has accomplished
    and study deeply what he has done.
10 Let all those restored to God's design of love rejoice in the Lord
    and rest secure in union with him;
    let all those with hearts set right with God praise him! ℞

Psalm 65
YOU HAVE THE REMEDY TO CLEANSE, HEAL AND RESTORE US

1   Because of you, O God, there is quiet rest and praise in Zion;
       what you have promised you have fulfilled.
2   Because you listen and understand what we truly need,
       people from all walks of life come to you.
3   Selfishness and fear—deviations from your design—overwhelm us,
       but you have the remedy to cleanse, heal and restore us.
4   You have chosen our health and happiness
       to bring us home—to live with you!
     You fill us with the goodness of your heavenly family
       to be part of your holy temple.
5   You have responded to our need in the most amazing way,
       O God, our Remedy, the source of eternal security for people the world over,
       even to the farthest seas.
6   You formed the mountains by your strength;
       you are encompassed with power and ability.
7   You calm the raging seas
       and the roaring waves, and the turmoil of the people.
8   Even people in the farthest reaches of the earth
       are awed by your wonderful works;
     what you have done brings songs of joy
       from one end of the earth to the other.
9   You sustain the earth and send rain to water it;
       you bring forth abundant life.
     God, you fill the streams with water to provide the earth with food.
       This is your design—how your law of love works:
10   From the oceans you send rain upon the plowed fields and soak them with water;
       you soften the soil with showers and cause the crops to grow.
11   At harvest you provide a rich bounty;
       wherever you go, life flourishes.
12   The pastures of the wilderness overflow with life;
       the hills, rich with vegetation, bring joy to the heart.
13   The meadows are covered with flocks
       and the valleys are full of grain;
       the entire world sings for joy. ⊗

PSALM 66
COME AND SEE WHAT GOD HAS DONE!

1   Joyfully praise God, all the earth!
2   Sing out the magnificence of his character of love;
        make glorious praises to him!
3   Proclaim to God, "Your works are awesome!
        Through your infinite love, through the weight of truth
    and the strength of your unchangeable design
        your enemies will bow down before you.
4   All the earth will bow down in your presence;
        they will sing praises to you—
        they will sing, praising your awesome character of love."
5   Come and see what God has done—
        see his amazing works for the good of humanity!
6   He removes obstacles: once he turned the sea into dry ground,
        and later the people walked through the river Jordan on foot—
        and we all rejoiced.
7   He governs forever,
        powerfully sustaining the laws upon which reality functions;
        he watches over the entire world and all its nations:
    but the rebellious—those who refuse God's methods—
        cannot heal themselves.
8   People everywhere, give our God the credit;
        let your praise for him be heard!
9   For he heals us, providing the cure to our terminal condition,
        and never seeks to trip us up.
10 For you, O God, examined us and diagnosed us,
        and then you cured us, making us pure like silver.
11 You left us free to wander from you and be trapped—
        our hearts weighed down by crushing affliction.
12 You allowed selfish people to trample over us;
        we have been burned by life
    and nearly drowned in a flood of problems,
        but you have rescued us and brought us to safety.
13 I will enter your house with self-sacrifice
        to fulfill my vow to you—

14   what I promised I would do,
         when I was in trouble.
15   I will symbolically enact my self-sacrifice and your plan to heal me
         by sacrificing fat animals to you, including rams, bulls and goats.
16   Come and listen, all you who are loyal to God,
         and I will tell you what he has done for me:
17   As I cried out to him for healing,
         I spoke clearly my praise for him.
18   If my heart had preferred to stay selfish,
         the Lord would not have listened to my words;
19   but God has most certainly listened
         and heard my heart's cry in my prayer.
20   All praise and honor be to God,
         who has not rejected my request for healing
         or withheld his transforming love from me! ৫

PSALM 67

YOU GUIDE THE PEOPLES BACK TO LIFE AND HEALTH

1   O God, show your favor toward us and heal us;
         cause your life-giving presence to shine upon us,
2   that your design for life and health may be known on earth
         and your healing remedy among all peoples.
3   May the nations thank you, O God;
         may all humanity give thanks to you!
4   May the peoples of the earth be glad and sing for joy,
         for you govern the world with absolute constancy,
     sustaining your design-laws,
         and you guide the peoples all over the world back to life and health.
5   May the nations of the earth thank you, O God;
         may all humanity give thanks to you!
6   Then the earth will yield its harvest of fully mature and righteous people,
         and God, our God, will bless us.
7   God will bless us,
         and the entire earth will honor and adore him. ৫

PSALM 68

EXALT HIM WHO RIDES ABOVE THE DESERTS OF LIFE

1 God springs into action, and his enemies scatter;
   those who hate love and truth flee from his presence.
2 As smoke is blown away by the wind,
   so the selfish are blown away by God's never-failing love;
as wax melts before the fire,
   so lies and liars are consumed by the fire of truth emanating from God.
3 But the healed—those whose hearts and minds are right with God—
   are glad and rejoice in God's presence:
   they are happy, healthy and joyful.
4 Sing to God, sing songs praising his character of love;
   exalt him who rides above the deserts of life,
exalt his character of love
   and rejoice in his presence!
5 As father to the fatherless and protector of widows,
   God lives in his holy dwelling place—in the Spirit temple.
6 God gathers those isolated by fear and selfishness
   and restores them to the family of God;
he frees those imprisoned by guilt and destructive habits,
   restoring them to life and health;
but those who persist in violating God's design
   wither—they remain severed from the source of life.
7 O God, when you led your people from slavery to freedom,
   when you marched through the wilderness,
8 the earth shook,
   the sky poured down rain
in the presence of the Creator—the self-existent One,
   the design-law-giver of Sinai;
   in the presence of the Creator—the God whom Israel trusted.
9 You gave abundant showers to the land
   and showers of truth and love to the people, O God;
they were tired and worn down
   and you revitalized them.
10 And life came to inhabit the land;
   for you, O Creator God,

from your goodness, provided for those who trusted you.

11 The Lord promised the healing solution,
and a great host of people spread the good news of God's remedy.

12 The king of war is banished—banished from land—
and the homeland shared the reward.

13 Even if we fall among the ashes,
the wings of the sacrificial dove
will purify us like silver and gold.

14 When the reign of the Almighty Creator spread throughout the land,
it healed it, covering the brokenness like pure-white snow.

15 The mountain of God replaces the mountains of self-exaltation[2]—
the mountains of self-exaltation that have many peaks.

16 O mountain of self-exaltation, why be envious
of the mountain where the God of love resides,
where the Creator God makes his home?

17 God's armies of angels are beyond counting—thousands upon thousands!
The Lord comes to dwell with humanity, just as he came at Sinai.

18 When you ascended to heaven,
you took those who were once captive in the grave,
and you procured the remedy for humanity (even for the rebellious),
that you, O Creator God, might dwell together with them.

19 May the Lord be praised!
Every day, the burden of our terminal condition is upon him,
for he is our remedy!

20 Our God is the only God who saves;
from the Creator God comes the remedy to escape eternal death.

21 God will unveil truth and love
which will destroy the fountainhead of his enemies—
the self-righteous crown of those who cling to lies and selfishness.

22 The Lord says, "I will bring them from their world of self-exaltation;
I will bring them back from the depths of the sea of sinfulness,

23 that you may reject their lies and crush their selfishness under your feet,
while the mouths of those evil ones confirm their terminal state."

24 The universe has seen how you conduct your affairs, O God;

---

2 The Hebrew original reads Bashan, which represents 'that which is the enemy to God' (see Psalms 22:12—'strong bulls of Bashan,' that are enemies to be consumed, as in Ezekiel 39:18).

the actions of my God and King
restore his perfect design of love into his sanctuary:

25 singers are in front, musicians in the rear,
with maidens in-between, playing tambourines—all in perfect harmony.

26 Praise God in the assembly of those with Godlike hearts;
praise the Lord in the assembly of those, who with God, overcome.

27 There, the least—like Benjamin—will be great,
and the leaders of Judah gather
along with the leaders of Zebulun and Naphtali.[3]

28 O God, command your power;
O God, command your power to work in our behalf!

29 Kings will bring presents to you—
to your temple at Jerusalem.

30 Rebuke the beastly, who, watching out for self, are unreliable like broken reeds;
the selfish mobs amass in droves like mindless bulls to stampede:
they stomp and trample, trying to force their way;
they offer bars of silver, trying to buy their way.
But God scatters those who delight in war.

31 Some will come to God from Egypt;
others, from Ethiopia, will bow in prayer to God.

32 Sing to God, O kingdoms of the earth,
sing praise to the Lord—

33 to him who from eternity-past rides over the heavens,
whose voice is like mighty thunder.

34 Tell everyone of the life-giving power of God
whose glorious character of love is reproduced in those,
who with him, overcome;
whose power sustains the universe.

35 O God, when you dwell in your living sanctuaries, it is truly awesome!
The God whom Israel trusted gives his live-giving power to his people.
All praise be to God! ᴔ

---

3 Hebrew names have associated meaning, thus providing an interpretive option to replace the proper noun with its denotation: Benjamin means "son of the right hand," Judah means "praise," Zebulon means "dwelling place" and "exalted" or "honored," and Naphtali means "my struggle, my strife." Hence, the passage could be rendered as:
"There my Son will sit at my right hand and rule,
and leaders will gather to praise—
leaders will dwell there, exalted and honored through struggle and strife."

Psalm 69

God will save his creation

1 Save me, O God,
   for I'm drowning in fear and sorrow, overwhelmed by anguish;
2 I'm sinking—it's like I'm in quicksand,
   with no solid footing.
   I'm in deep water—
   the waves of heartache engulf me.
3 I'm exhausted, worn out from crying for help;
   my throat is raw,
   my eyes are swollen from weeping—
   I'm waiting for my God to help.
4 Those who hate me without cause or reason
   outnumber the hairs on my head;
   powerful are my enemies,
   who without cause want to destroy me with their lies.
   That which I did not take
   I must now restore.
5 O God, you know when I have been foolish—
   my deviations from your design for life are not hidden from you.
6 Do not let those who trust in you
   be disgraced because of me,
   O Lord God Almighty;
   do not let those who seek you
   be ashamed because of me,
   O God of the victorious.
7 I bear scorn for your cause
   in order to overcome the shame that lies before me.
8 I am like a stranger to my own family,
   an alien to my own siblings.
9 A passionate desire to complete God's healing plan
   and restore God's house consumes me;
   I accept the abuse meant for you,
   in order to protect and heal you.
10 My heartache and fasting

are mocked and ridiculed;
11 when I put on ashes—my clothes of mourning—
    they made jokes about me.
12 Church and city leaders make fun of me,
    and drunkards jeer me in song.
13 But I pray to you, O Lord,
    for the time of acceptance;
  O God of love and goodness,
    answer me with your saving remedy.
14 Rescue me from the miry pit,
    do not let me sink into despair;
  deliver me from those who hate me,
    don't let me drown in the flood of sorrows.
15 Do not let the waves of anguish engulf me
    or the depths of darkness devour me;
    don't let the grave consume me.
16 O Lord, respond with your glorious goodness and love;
    with your infinite mercy and tenderness, take care of me.
17 Please don't put me on hold—don't make me wait to see you;
    answer my call quickly, for I am in real trouble.
18 Touch me and heal me,
    rescue me from my enemies.
19 You know how I am mocked, shamed and humiliated;
    you see all my enemies and how they mistreat me.
20 Slander, scorn and rejection have broken my heart;
    such animosity and callousness sicken me.
  I look for sympathy, but there is none,
    for someone to comfort me, but I found no one.
21 They gave me poison for food
    and vinegar to quench my thirst.
22 May what they rely on for strength and sustenance
    be revealed as a snare and a trap—
    the actual cause of their stumbling and the source of their pain.
23 May their rejection of truth damage their minds so they no longer comprehend,
    and may their characters be so twisted by persistent rebellion

       that they will not reform.

24   Pour out your heartbreaking disappointment in them;
       may they know how losing them eternally angers you.

25   Allow them to have what they have chosen—
       may their land be empty and their homes lifeless.

26   For they injure those whom you are working to heal
       and make fun of the pain of those who follow your treatment plan.

27   Let their terminal condition confirm
       that they persist in deviating from your design—
       that they refuse your healing remedy.

28   Their individualities will be erased from the heavenly archive of life—
       they will not be found among the eternally healed.

29   I am suffering and hurting;
       may your perfect remedy, O God, restore me.

30   My life will be a song of praise to God's character of love;
       I will magnify his character of love with thanksgiving.

31   Transformed lives please the Lord more than ritual offering—
       much more than any ceremonial sacrifices.

32   When the meek see this reality, they will rejoice,
       for those who seek God will have their hearts healed!

33   The Lord responds to those who know their need and call to him;
       he does not reject people born captive in sin.

34   Let heaven and earth praise him,
       and the sea and all creatures in them,

35   for God will save his creation
       and rebuild the earth into perfection.
       Then human beings will live on the new earth and possess it;

36   *the children of his loyal followers will inherit it,*
   and those who love his character and methods of love
       will dwell there forever. ❧

PSALM 70

YOU ARE MY HELP AND MY CURE

1   Act now, O God, to heal me;
    O Lord, come quickly to help me!
2   Those who seek to kill me will reap shame and humiliation;
    all who desire my ruin will run away in disgrace.
3   Those who say, "Aha, we've got him now!"
    will be crushed by their own shame.
4   But all who seek you and your methods
    will rejoice and be glad when united with you;
all those who love your healing remedy will proclaim,
    "The Creator God is great!"
5   Yet I am terminal and need your remedy;
    come quickly to me, O God.
You are my help and my cure;
    O Lord, come quickly and heal me! ❧

Psalm 71

Your right and perfect character is the praise of heaven

1 O Lord, I trust you completely;
     take away all my shame.
2 Recreate me and restore me to your perfect and righteous design;
     hear me and save me from fear and selfishness.
3 Be my remedy and my recovery room
     to which I can always go;
   give the command to heal me,
     for you are my remedy and my refuge.
4 Set me free, O God, from fear and selfishness,
     from the clutches of evil and cruelty.
5 For you, O Creator God, are my only hope,
     the source of my confidence since my youth.
6 I have relied on you since birth;
     you have provided for me since the day I was born.
     I live in continual praise to you.
7 To many, my life is evidence of your saving power,
     because upon you I have relied for healing and restoration.
8 Praise for you constantly pours from my mouth;
     I proclaim the beauty of your character of love all day long.
9 Do not force me to retire when I am old;
     do not release me from your service when my strength is gone.
10 My enemies misrepresent me;
     they conspire together, watching for an opportunity to destroy me.
11 They say, "God has abandoned him;
     take him down now,
     for no one will rescue him."
12 O God, don't stay away a moment longer than necessary;
     come quickly to help me, O my God.
13 My accusers will be consumed with shame;
     those who want to destroy me
     will drown in their humiliation and disgrace.
14 But I will continually trust you
     and praise you with ever greater affection and regard.

¹⁵ I will tell of your right and holy character and methods of love;
  all day long I will speak of your remedy to fear and selfishness,
even though the magnitude of your achievement
  is beyond my comprehension.
¹⁶ I will go empowered by you, O Creator God;
  I will promote your character and methods of love, and only yours!
¹⁷ O Creator God, you have taught me of your kingdom of love
  since my childhood,
  and to this day I proclaim how wonderful you are!
¹⁸ And even when I am old and gray,
  do not release me from your service, O God;
empower me to proclaim your kingdom of love to the next generation—
  the power of your healing remedy to those who come after me.
¹⁹ Your right and perfect character of love, O God, is the praise of heaven;
  you have done great things
  and there is none like you!
²⁰ You have shown me the selfishness within me—
  the source of my pain and sorrow;
you bring to me your life-giving remedy,
  and from the grave you will raise me to everlasting life.
²¹ You make me greater, healthier, holier and happier than ever before
  and surround me with your comforting presence.
²² I will praise you with song
  for your never-changing love and goodness, O my God;
my life will be a song of praise to you,
  O Holy One, in whom Israel trusted.
²³ I will shout for joy and sing your praises,
  for you have healed me!
²⁴ I will tell of your perfect character of love
  for all eternity,
for those who sought to destroy me
  reap only shame and humiliation. ∽

Psalm 72

You are Designer and Builder of All Reality

1   Give the king the knowledge of your design-law, O God,
      imbue him with your perfect character of love and truth.
2   Enable him to govern in harmony with your righteous principles
      and to share your right remedy with those suffering in sin.
3   Then the temple-mount will be a place of healing to the people—
      the places of worship will promote your righteous character.
4   The king will advocate for the poor and afflicted
      and give remedy to those who need it;
      his perfect character of love will crush the selfish oppressor.
5   The people will revere you, O God, as creator of sun and moon,
      as designer and builder of all reality,
      through all generations.
6   The king will bring life—like refreshing rain to a mown lawn,
      like showers that water the earth.
7   From his life, the righteous will blossom and grow—
      an abundant harvest of spiritually-healthy people
      ever increasing until the dark night of sin is past.
8   He will reign from sea to sea,
      from the river Euphrates to the ends of the earth.
9   The people from the entire earth—even from its remotest parts—
      will kneel before him
    and his enemies, consumed with guilt and shame,
      will hide their faces in the dirt to evade his gaze.
10 The rulers of the western nations and distant lands will bring him gifts;
      the monarchs of the eastern and southern nations
      will present him their offerings.
11 All heads-of-state will bow down before him,
      and all nations will serve him.
12 For he will rescue the needy when they turn to him
      and heal the broken-hearted who choose him as their only remedy.
13 He will be merciful to the weak—those who recognize their spiritual need—
      and heal them from their sin-sick terminal condition.
14 He will deliver them from the oppression and violence of selfishness,

for their lives are very precious to him.
15 He will be Life—the healing remedy to cure the infection of sin;
    he will provide the gold of a perfect righteous character of love.
May the people keep in constant communion with him—
    praising, valuing and adoring him continually.
16 Let the seeds of truth blossom throughout the world;
    in every high place of worship may they flourish.
Let the fruit of righteousness abound like the forests of Lebanon,
    thriving like grass of the field.
17 His character of love will endure forever,
    the fame of his perfection—longer than the sun.
The human race will be blessed by him,
    and they will call him "the Blessed One."
18 All praise to our Creator God—the God whom Israel trusted—
    who alone does what is marvelous.
19 Praise be to his glorious character of love forever;
    may the whole earth be filled with his life-giving glory.
    So let it always be!
20 (This concludes the prayers of David, son of Jesse). ❧

Psalm 73

God is my Remedy — My Source of Eternal Life

1 We know that God is good to the upright—
    to those who are pure in heart.
2 But I almost tripped myself up;
    I nearly slipped away from the truth:
3 I began to envy the arrogant
    when I saw how the selfish prospered in this world.
4 They don't suffer with physical disabilities;
    their bodies are strong and healthy.
5 They are privileged—not burdened with the problems of ordinary people;
    they do not have the daily struggles that others endure.
6 Their pride and arrogance are flaunted like a necklace;
    violence and exploitation cover them.
7 They go about draped in extravagant riches,
    intoxicating themselves with whatever their selfish hearts can imagine.
8 They belittle others and speak harmful words designed to injure;
    they exalt themselves, lording over others and threatening oppression.
9 They claim to speak for heaven,
    and with their decrees they seek to rule the earth.
10 People turn to them
    and sadly, have the water of life drained away from them.
11 These haughty ones say, "God will not know.
    The Most High will not find out."
12 Look at what the selfish are like:
    concerned only with self, they get richer and richer.
13 I wondered, "Has my pure living been for nothing?
    Did I keep myself innocent for no reason?
14 All day long I am touched by problems and temptation;
    every day is a struggle."
15 If I had shared these ideas as truths with others,
    I would have betrayed all who are loyal to you.
16 When I tried to understand why the selfish seem to prosper,
    it made no sense to me
17 until I studied the lessons revealed in the holy places of God:

then I understood their inevitable end.

18 Truly you gave them the freedom to slip around your design for life;
     you surrender them to their own terminal condition.

19 Their desolation is swift—
     they are consumed completely
     by the terrors of unremedied selfishness.

20 Selfish success is like a dream when one awakes:
     When the Creator restores earth to his design of love,
     all will realize that selfish prosperity is mere fantasy.

21 When my heart was sour,
     discontented and torn up inside,

22 I was ignorant and didn't understand reality at all;
     I must have seemed like a dumb animal to you.

23 Nevertheless, I have always stayed close to you,
     and you hold my hand as I journey through life.

24 With your wise counsel, you lead me in the way of life
     to the complete restoration of your glory within me.

25 There is nothing in all the heavens
     or anything on earth that I desire besides you.

26 My mind and body may grow weak,
     but God is my remedy—
     my source of eternal life.

27 Those who separate from you will perish;
     all who choose selfishness betray you and your kingdom of love—
     they will be severed from life and cease to exist.

28 But as for me, being united with God is my greatest delight—
     to find healing and restoration with my Creator,
     and to proclaim all that you have done! ❧

Psalm 74

By Overthrowing Death, You Bring Life to the Earth

1   What happened, O God, that you left us to our own devices?
     It seems like you have been gone forever!
     Are you angry with your chosen helpers?

2   Remember the people you chose long ago—
     whom you freed from slavery to be the conduit of your remedy—
     and Mount Zion, where you once dwelt.

3   Run and see the totality of the destruction,
     all the damage the enemy has done to your sanctuary.

4   In the heart of your temple, your foes roared their defiance of your ways;
     they set up their standards where yours should be kept.

5   They wielded their axes like lumberjacks,
     as if they were cutting down a forest of trees.

6   All the wood paneling they demolished
     with their axes and crowbars.

7   They set your sanctuary on fire;
     they desecrated your tabernacle, tearing it down to the ground.

8   They said to themselves, "We will beat them into total submission!"
     They burned down every place where God was worshipped.

9   We saw no sign from heaven;
     none of your spokespersons are left,
     and no one knows how long this will last.

10 How long, O God, will the enemy ridicule and mock you?
     Will the adversary despise your character of love forever?

11 Why do you tie your hands; why do you hold back your power?
     Let loose your power, and the enemy will be destroyed!

12 But you, O Creator God, are my eternal King;
     by overthrowing death, you bring life to the earth.

13 You parted the sea by your mighty power;
     in the midst of turmoil that raged like angry seas,
     you smashed the dragon's head.

14 It was you who crushed the head of the great serpent,
     leaving the meat of his lies, fear and selfishness
     for those who chose death in the desert.

15 You broke open the streams of life-giving water;
        you made the river a dry road to a new land.
16 You created both the day and the night;
        you put the sun and moon in their place.
17 You designed and built earth, establishing all the parameters for life;
        you created time with its changing seasons.
18 Remember, O Creator God, how the enemy demeans you,
        how the foolish revile your character of love
        and your design-law for life.
19 Do not leave your helpless children, like doves, to the beastly;
        do not let your suffering helpers forget you forever.
20 Focus on your promised remedy,
        because the earth is sick:
        every corner is filled with darkness and violence.
21 Don't bring the afflicted home in disgrace;
        may the humble who know their need
        come home radiating your glorious character of love.
22 Rise up, O God, and advance your remedy of truth and love;
        remember how the foolish ridicule you all day long.
23 Do not let the lies of your enemies go unanswered—
        the constant roar of their false allegations which arise continually. ଓ

Psalm 75

The Power of Truth and Love Will Be Exalted

1 We give thanks to you, O Creator God,
   we give thanks, for your character of love fills our hearts;
   we proclaim the beauty of your wonderful ways.

2 God says, "When the time is right,
   I will unite with my people
   and govern them uprightly.

3 When the earth and all its selfish inhabitants slowly decay,
   it is I who holds the cure—the foundational design for life.

4 To the arrogant I say, 'Stop bragging about yourselves—you have no remedy,'
   and to the wicked, 'Do not blow your own horn of self-exaltation.

5 Do not trumpet your own spiritual health, trying to exalt yourselves;
   do not be proud, with heads held high
   and necks unwilling to bend in humility and accept treatment.'"

6 The exaltation and restoration of humanity
   does not come from anywhere on earth—
   east or west, north or south.

7 It is the Creator God who governs!
   The proudly-selfish die, while the humbly-righteous live.

8 In the hand of the Lord is a cup
   filled with the unfermented wine of absolute truth and love;
   he pours it out, and all the selfish of the earth
   drink down the truth of their true condition,
   bitterly swallowing every evil and corrupt fact they have thus far denied.

9 As for me, I will proclaim this forever;
   I will sing praises to the God whom Israel trusted.

10 God will destroy fear and selfishness—the power of the wicked—
   but the power of truth and love will be exalted. ෬

PSALM 76

FROM HEAVEN, HE ACCURATELY DIAGNOSES OUR CONDITION

1   God has revealed himself in Judah;
        his character of love is powerfully proclaimed in Israel.
2   His embassy—his refuge on earth—is in Salem.
3   There he destroys the fiery arrows of the evil one;
        he provides the shield of trust and the sword of truth—
        his weapons of war.
4   You are radiant with truth and love,
        a magnificent mountain of selflessness—
        a Lamb led to slaughter.
5   The soldiers of selfishness lie ravaged,
        they sleep in death;
    not one of their warriors
        can raise a hand.
6   At your loving rebuke, O God of Jacob,
        the engines of destruction cease.
7   You are awe-inspiring, the only One to be revered.
        Who can stand in your presence without your consent?
8   From heaven, you accurately diagnosed their terminal condition—
        the people are stunned and stand silent
9   when you, O God, rise up to pronounce your diagnosis
        and heal the humble people of earth.
10 Truly, humanity's rebellion and rage confirm your diagnosis,
        as you take their venom and hostility upon yourself.
11 Commit yourself to the Lord your God and fulfill your commitment;
        surround him with gifts and reverent devotion.
12 His truth and love humble proud princes;
        the haughty kings of the earth fear him. ೞ

Psalm 77

You Are the God Who Built Reality Itself

1 I cry out to God—Help me, please help me!
      I cry out to God—O hear my plea!
2 When I was in trouble, overwhelmed and afraid, I ran to the Lord;
      all night I prayed with my hands reaching out toward heaven,
      but my heart resisted his comfort.
3 I thought of you—your methods of love and truth—and I groaned;
      I brooded, clinging to my selfish desires,
      and I became even more overwhelmed.
4 You opened my eyes to my true condition;
      it was so upsetting I couldn't talk about it.
5 My thoughts went back to better times,
      to years long ago;
6 at night I remembered my songs from the past.
      My heart searched deeply;
      my mind thought intensely about the differences.
7 "Will the Lord let me go my own way forever?
      Will he never be pleased with my choices again?
8 Has his perfect love disappeared from my heart completely?
      Has his promise to heal me been permanently hindered?
9 Has God forgotten his merciful plan?
      Has he given up on me and withheld his remedy?"
10 It sickens me to think that I could obstruct
      the plan of the Creator God to heal me.
11 I will change my focus and remember the works of the Lord;
      yes, I will remember the amazing things you did long ago.
12 I will meditate on your achievements—your methods of love and truth;
      I will consider the meaning of all you have done.
13 Your methods, O Creator God, are holy—the perfect design for life.
      No god is as great as you!
14 You are the God who built the universe—the creator of reality itself;
      you have revealed your power over nature to the entire world.
15 With your great might you delivered your helpers—
      the descendants of Jacob and Joseph.

¹⁶ The waters encountered you, O God,
  the waters encountered you and awaited your command;
  the very depths of the sea convulsed at your bidding.
¹⁷ The clouds poured down rain,
  thunder rumbled through the sky, and lightning flashed back and forth.
¹⁸ Your voice was like thunder from heaven,
  your presence like lightning brightening the world;
  the earth trembled and quaked at your approach.
¹⁹ You walked right through the sea,
  forging a path through the raging waters, though you left no footprints.
²⁰ You led your helpers like a flock of sheep,
  with Moses and Aaron as their shepherds.

PSALM 78

HE FORGIVES AND LONGS TO HEAL OUR SIN-SICK CONDITION

1 Pay close attention, my people, to my instructions;
    listen carefully to what I have to say.
2 I will teach in parables,
    revealing truths obscured since the creation of the world,
3 explaining the meaning of things we have all heard about—
    the things our ancestors have told us.
4 We will not conceal these truths from our children;
    we will tell the next generation
of God's glorious character of love,
    his fierce goodness, and the magnificent things he has done.
5 He provided a script to teach Israel his healing plan
    and establish in them his design protocols for life
which he commanded our ancestors
    to teach to their children—
6 so that the next generation would share in his remedy—
    and to the children of theirs, yet to be born,
    who would in turn share the remedy with their own children.
7 Then they would put their complete trust in God,
    remember how he works—applying methods of love and truth—
    and live in harmony with his design for life.
8 Then they would not end up like their ancestors—
    callous, hard-hearted and uncured,
with selfish hearts disloyal to God
    and minds that did not know or trust him.
9 The descendants of Ephraim, though armed with the arrows of truth,
    turned back to paganism when the battle with idolatry came;
10 they did not follow the script—the healing plan—
    and refused to live in harmony with God's design for life.
11 They forgot the evidence he had provided—
    the wonderful manifestation of himself to them:
12 He wrought miracles in the sight of their ancestors living in the Zoan,
    which exposed the gods of Egypt as false;
13 he parted the sea and led them through,
    making the waters stand firm like walls;

¹⁴ he guided them from a cloud by day
and from a pillar of fire by night;
¹⁵ he caused the desert rocks to burst open
and gave them water from the depths of the earth;
¹⁶ he caused streams to rush out of the rock
and made their water flow like a river.
¹⁷ But they continued to distrust God,
rebelling in the desert against the Most High Creator
and pursuing their own selfish desires instead.
¹⁸ They rejected God's plan and gave him an ultimatum:
they demanded the food their unhealthy appetites craved.
¹⁹ They murmured against God, saying,
"Can't God give us decent food here in the desert?
²⁰ Sure, he struck the rock and plenty of water gushed out,
but can he give us a proper meal—the meat that we crave?"
²¹ When the Lord heard that they rejected his healing plan,
he was very dismayed;
he released his fire of truth and evidence upon the people
and set them free to experience what they demanded,
²² since they did not believe God
or trust in his treatment plan.
²³ Even though he had commanded the skies to open
and had unlocked the storehouse of heaven,
²⁴ and rained down manna for the people to eat
and gave them bread from heaven;
²⁵ even though the people ate the bread of angels
and had more food than they could eat,
²⁶ he let them have their way and loosed the east wind
and sent the south wind as well.
²⁷ Meat rained down on them like dust—
birds flew in, plentiful like sands on the seashore.
²⁸ The birds fell all throughout the camp,
all around their tents.
²⁹ They ate until they could eat no more,
for he had given them over to their uncontrolled cravings.
³⁰ Before they finished gorging themselves,

while they were still chewing,
31 what God was grieved about, happened to them:
the most gluttonous among them died;
the chosen people of Israel were cut down.
32 In spite of this evidence that deviating from God's design destroys,
they refused to trust him and kept on choosing selfishness;
they did not believe in his wonderful ways.
33 So their days were useless, expended in futility;
consumed by fear, they died in the desert.
34 But others saw what had happened and they sought God;
they turned around and said they would follow him.
35 They remembered that God was their refuge and remedy,
that the Creator God was their salvation.
36 But their words of commitment were false,
their declarations of love and devotion were lies;
37 their hearts were not changed—they were not loyal to him,
so they did not trust him or follow his treatment plan.
38 Yet he was compassionate and merciful;
he forgave them and longed to heal their sin-sick condition,
and he did not destroy them.
He gave them countless opportunities to be renewed
and did not leave them to their own devices forever.
39 He remembered that they were mere mortals
with lives like a breeze, that quickly pass by.
40 Too often they refused his help in the desert—
much grief they caused him in the wilderness!
41 Again and again they tested God's patience;
they worked against his healing plan, frustrating the Holy One of Israel.
42 They had no appreciation for what he had done for them;
they forgot that he delivered them from slavery
43 and miraculously exposed the gods of Egypt as false—
the powerful evidences presented in Zoan.
44 He turned their rivers into blood,
and their false gods could not give them water to drink from their streams.
45 He sent biting insects to unsettle their distorted beliefs,
and frogs that overran their land.

46 He sent locust to destroy their crops—
   evidence that without him, their labor was fruitless.
47 He destroyed their vines with hail,
   and with freezing rain shattered their fig trees.
48 He rained hail upon their cattle
   and sent lightning strikes upon their livestock.
49 He let loose his anger at the lies that held them captive;
   he revealed his wrath and rage at the sin-sickness that held them in bondage;
   he sent angels with power to expose the lies and reveal him as their remedy.
50 He made a therapeutic intervention—a way for the sin-sickness to be defeated;
   those who refused his remedy, he did not prevent from dying,
   but gave the rebellious over to their terminal choice.
51 He put the firstborn of the hostile Egyptians to sleep in the grave—
   the firstfruits of the procreative power of the descendants of Ham.
52 But he led his helpers out like a flock of sheep,
   guiding them safely through the wilderness.
53 He protected them, so they were not afraid,
   but the sea drowned their enemies.
54 Thus he brought them to the border of the land he set apart for them—
   to the Mount he reclaimed for the manifestation
   of his power of truth and love.
55 He drove out the nations before them
   and divided the land, giving each tribe their portion;
   he let the tribes of Israel settle into their tents.
56 But they tested whether God and his methods were true—
   they rebelled against the Creator God and his intent;
   they did not follow his treatment plan.
57 Like their ancestors, they were non-compliant and refused his remedy;
   warped in their thinking, they were as unreliable as a crooked bow.
58 They distressed him with their false remedies;
   they aroused his passion to help them understand
   what they were really doing to themselves by worshipping false gods.
59 When God heard that they preferred their sickness to his cure,
   he was very distressed and stepped back completely,
   letting Israel experience what they had themselves chosen.
60 He departed from the little theater-sanctuary at Shiloh—

the tent he had set up to teach the people of his healing plan.

61 Without his presence, the ark—the symbol of restored unity with God—
  was taken away from them;
  the emblem of his splendid healing plan
  was captured by their adversaries.

62 He surrendered them to their own treatment program
  and they were destroyed by their enemies.
  He was very angry at what his helpers inflicted upon themselves.

63 Their young men were killed in war,
  so their young women had no men to marry.

64 Their priests, who peddled a false remedy, were slaughtered,
  and their widows had no time to mourn.

65 When enough evidence had been revealed,
  the Lord rose up like a person aroused from a sleep,
  like a warrior awakening from a stuporous grief.

66 He beat back the enemies of truth and love—the purveyors of false remedies—
  yet they remained unhealed;
  he gave them over to shame that they could not escape.

67 He refused to place the tabernacle amongst Joseph's descendants;
  he did not choose the tribe of Ephraim.

68 To reveal his love,
  he chose the tribe of Judah at Mount Zion.

69 There he built his temple to restore humanity to his highest perfection
  and establish himself on earth by becoming one of us, forever. [4]

70 He chose David as his agent and human ancestor
  and brought him from the sheep pens,

71 from tending ewes and lambs,
  to be king of Israel—the shepherd of God's people.

72 David cared for them with sincerity—with a heart desiring to do what is right—
  and he led them skillfully. ଔ

---

[4] The paraphrase takes the position that the temple referred to in this passage is more than the building of stone built by Solomon and refers to the ultimate temple that Jesus built and to which Solomon's temple only pointed: "Tell him this is what the Lord Almighty says: 'Here is the man whose name is the Branch, and he will branch out from his place and build the temple of the Lord. It is he who will build the temple of the Lord, and he will be clothed with majesty and will sit and rule on his throne. And he will be a priest on his throne. And there will be harmony between the two.'" (Zechariah 6:12,13). This is the temple to which Jesus referred when he said, "Destroy this temple, and I will raise it again in three days." (John 2:19 NIV). It is the temple of Jesus' humanity that He perfected in sinlessness in order to be our remedy.

PSALM 79
MAY YOUR CHARACTER OF LOVE BE MAGNIFIED

1 O God, the selfish have invaded the land where you chose to reveal your remedy;
  they have defiled the little theater-temple
set apart to teach your healing plan,
  and they have reduced Jerusalem to rubble.

2 They have left for the vultures the corpses of your helpers,
  and the bodies of your friends to be devoured by wild beasts.

3 The blood they have shed runs down the streets of Jerusalem like water,
  and there is no one to bury the dead.

4 The other nations look down upon us;
  they ridicule us, mock us and make jokes about us.

5 How long, O Lord, will this go on?
  Will you leave us to our own devices forever?
  How long must your fiery truth burn before we finally learn?

6 Let the selfish nations go—those who do not know you;
  let go of the kingdoms
  that do not value your character of love,

7 for they have feasted on Israel—devouring their innocence—
  and have destroyed their families.

8 Do not hold against us the self-destructive choices of our ancestors,
  but send to us quickly your tender compassion—your healing remedy—
  for we are in desperate need.

9 Help us, O God our Savior,
  so that your character of love may be exalted in the universe;
deliver us from selfishness and fix all deviations from your design within us,
  so that your character of love may be magnified.

10 Why should the nations wonder
  if our Creator God is true?
Let us watch as the nations learn that they cannot escape reality
  of the destructive results of killing your helpers who spread your remedy.

11 May those suffering from fear and selfishness cry out to you;
  may your powerful remedy heal and restore the terminal—
those condemned to die because they are out of harmony
  with your design for life.

¹² To the hearts of our selfish neighbors,
>   return all the lies and insults they have hurled at you, O Lord.
¹³ Then we, the people who trust and follow you like sheep their shepherd,
>   will praise you forever and ever;
>   we will proclaim your greatness for all generations. ❧

PSALM 80
RESTORE US TO YOUR PERFECT DESIGN, O CREATOR GOD

¹ Hear us, O Shepherd of those, who like Israel, cling to God;
>   may you increase those whom you lead.⁵
> You sit enthroned above the mightiest angels;
>   shine forth the radiance of your truth and love
² into the hearts of your people,
>   that they may be fruitful, powerful in your cause,
> and forget their selfish ways.⁶
>   Display your recreative power and heal us.
³ Restore us to your perfect design, O Creator God;
>   make your flawless character of love shine upon us,
>   that we may be healed to be like you.
⁴ O Lord God Almighty,
>   how long will our foolish requests frustrate your healing plan?
⁵ We fill ourselves with sorrow
>   and drown in our tears.
⁶ You let us become hated by our neighbors
>   and ridiculed by our enemies.
⁷ Restore us to your perfect design, O Creator God;
>   make your flawless character of love shine upon us,
>   that we may be healed to be like you.
⁸ You brought us out of Egypt like a grapevine;
>   you drove out the devouring forces and planted us in the land.

---

⁵ In this place, the Hebrew original writings use the name Joseph, which means "may Jehovah give increase," and in this verse, the meaning of the name is utilized.

⁶ In this place, the Hebrew original writings use the names Ephraim, which means "fruitful;" Benjamin, which means "son of right hand" or "power;" and Manasseh, which means "causing to forget." In this verse, the meanings of the names are utilized.

⁹ You prepared a place for us to grow,
 and we set down roots and filled the land.
¹⁰ The shade of our prosperity stretched over the countryside;
 our family tree's branches are strong like the mighty cedars.
¹¹ We branched out to the Mediterranean
 and grew to reach the Euphrates river.
¹² What was it that broke down our protective hedge
 so that any who pass by can steal our offspring?
¹³ Like wild pigs they trample us;
 like vermin they leech off of us.
¹⁴ Almighty Creator God, come back to us and restore your protection;
 look down from heaven, see what is wrong,
 and give your people the help they need.
¹⁵ Come and revive the grapevine you planted—
 this branch of humanity's family tree
 that you have chosen for the outworking of your healing plan.
¹⁶ You have burned away the dross and pruned back the dead branches;
 at your rebuke, selfishness is destroyed.
¹⁷ Give your power and authority to the One who stands at your right hand—
 to the Son of Man you have raised up as your Remedy.
¹⁸ Then we will not turn away from you:
 give us life—your healing remedy—
 and we will proclaim your character of love.
¹⁹ Restore us to your perfect design, O Creator God;
 make your flawless character of love shine upon us,
 that we may be healed to be like you. ♋

PSALM 81

"I HAVE LIFTED THE BURDEN FROM YOU"

1 Sing the joyous strains about God our refuge and remedy;
  proclaim your praise to the God who transformed Jacob!

2 Begin the musical score, strike the tambourine,
  play the melodious story on harp and lyre.

3 Blow the trumpet at the New Moon,
  and when the moon is full,
  to start our recurring celebratory enactment—

4 this is a script for the descendants of Israel,
  a direction from the God who transformed Jacob.

5 He established this as a prescription for the descendants of Israel,
  when he attacked the false beliefs promoted in Egypt,
  in order to set us free.
  There we heard a voice we did not recognize, saying,

6 "I have lifted the burden from you;
  I have set you free.

7 When you were distressed and called on me, I saved you,
  I answered you from the thundercloud;
  I gave you the opportunity to exercise and strengthen your trust in me
  when I provided water for you at Meribah.

8 "Listen to me, my people, and I will tell you the way of life—
  O that you would follow my prescription!

9 You must never allow false gods to infect your understanding;
  you must never trust them or surrender your hearts to them.

10 I am the Creator, your God
  who set you free from the bondage of Egypt.
  Hunger for truth, righteousness and mature character,
  and I will fill you.

11 But my people refused to listen to me;
  they would not follow my prescription.

12 So I let them go the way on which their stubborn hearts insisted
  to fulfill their own selfish desires.

13 If my people would simply follow my prescription,
  if they would embrace the truth

and live in harmony with my design for life,

14 I would quickly silence all enemies
   and use my healing power against all destructive forces.

15 Those who hate me and reject my remedy cower before me,
   and their terminal condition will never be cured.

16 But you who trust me will be fed with the bread of life;
   with the honey of perfection that comes from the rock, I will heal you." ℚ

PSALM 82

RISE UP, O GOD, AND DIAGNOSE THE EARTH

1 God takes a stand against the assembly of false gods;
   he presents his diagnosis regarding all pagan gods.

2 He says, "When will you stop using a list of rules to govern?
   When will you stop protecting selfishness with your legal system?

3 Do what is actually right, healthy and loving for all people;
   protect the poor and the fatherless;
   do what is right to the poor and oppressed—what heals and restores.

4 Rescue the weak and needy;
   deliver them from the power of selfishness.

5 These false gods don't understand reality;
   they don't understand my design-laws—how I built life to function;
   they operate in the darkness of a rule-enforcement system
   and the world is crumbling all around them.

6 I say to you, fallen angels pretending to be gods,
   "Even though you are all children of the Most High,

7 you will die like mortals;
   your life will end like that of any ordinary ruler."

8 Rise up, O God, and diagnose the earth,
   for the entire world belongs to you. ℚ

PSALM 83

O GOD, DO NOT REST FROM YOUR REDEMPTIVE WORK

1   O God, do not rest from your redemptive work,
>   do not be at peace while selfishness rages;
>   O Creator God, do not stop opposing evil.

2   Look at the confusion and uproar your enemies create
>   and see how those who hate you rebel against love and truth.

3   They connive and plot to destroy your helpers;
>   they conspire to destroy those through whom your precious remedy is given.

4   "Come," they say, "let us destroy the entire nation,
>   so that the remedy that transformed Israel will be completely forgotten."

5   With hearts united in selfishness, they agree on their plan;
>   they form an alliance against you and your methods of love.

6   Those who oppose your remedy include the people of Edom and the Ishmaelites,
>   the Moabites and Hagrites,

7   the people of Gebal, Ammon and Amalek,
>   the Philistines and the people of Tyre.

8   Assyria has also joined them,
>   uniting with the Ammonites and Moabites, the descendants of Lot.

9   Do not let them succeed,
>   as you did not let the false gods of Midian succeed,
>   as you did not let Sisera and Jabin succeed at the river Kishon—

10   they died at Endor
>   and their corpses became manure for the ground.

11   Let those who refuse your remedy
>   be like the Midianite generals Oreb and Zeeb;
>   let them reap the death they have chosen—
>   like the Midianite kings Zebah and Zalmunna,

12   who, choosing selfishness over love, said,
>   "Let us take for ourselves the land God has chosen."

13   Let them be like tumbleweed, O my God,
>   dispersed like chaff before the wind.

14   As fire consumes the forest,
>   may the flames of truth burn down their mountain of self-sufficient lies,

15 may the storms of life overtake them,
      may the swirling tempest of their selfish hearts terrify them.
16 May they see themselves as they truly are and be ashamed,
      so that people will seek your character of love, O Creator God.
17 These unhealed will know only humiliation and terror;
      they will die in disgrace.
18 They will begrudgingly acknowledge that you alone are God—
      that you are the Most High, the Creator and Sustainer of the entire earth. ⌇

PSALM 84

HEALTHY AND HAPPY IS THE ONE WHO TRUSTS IN YOU

1 How I love your sanctuary—your dwelling place—
   O Creator God!

2 My inmost self desperately craves your presence—
   to be in the courts where you dwell;
   my heart, my body—my entire being cries out
   for the God of life.

3 Even the sparrow has a home,
   and the swallow a nest for herself,
   where she may care for her young—near your altar,
   O Creator and Sustainer of all, my King and my God.

4 Oh, what health and happiness for those who live in your house—
   lives of constant love and praise for you.

5 What health and happiness for those whose strength comes from you—
   who set their hearts on finding you.

6 As they pass through life's valley of sorrows,
   you make it a place of renewal with life-giving springs;
   the rains become refreshing pools.

7 They gain strength with each victory in life,
   until they appear before God in Zion.

8 O Lord, Mighty Creator God, hear my prayer;
   listen to me, O God whom Jacob trusted.

9 Take notice of our shield—the King;
   look favorably upon your Anointed One.

10 Better is one day spent in the courts where you dwell
    than a thousand away from you;
    I would rather stand at the entrance to the house of my God
    than live in comfort in the tents of the wicked.

11 For the Lord God is our life-giving sun and our protective shield,
    providing continual grace to transform us to his glorious ideal;
    he will withhold nothing that is good
    from those who choose to live in harmony with his design.

12 O Creator God,
    healthy and happy is the person who trusts in you. ○○

Psalm 85

Love and Truth Are Perfectly United

1 You have revealed your merciful plan in your land, O Lord;
   you set captive Israel free.
2 You have taken the sin-sickness of humanity upon yourself
   and provided the remedy to erase all deviations from your design.
3 You come to us with your love;
   you smile upon us with your mercy.
4 Restore us completely, O God our Savior,
   and stay close to us.
5 Will you allow our lack of cooperation to keep you away forever?
   Will you leave us to ourselves for all generations?
6 Will you not heal our hearts again,
   that we might live to love and rejoice in you?
7 O Lord, pour upon us your life-giving love,
   and grant us your eternal healing.
8 I will do what the Lord God says,
   following all his prescriptions;
   he provides peace and wellness
   to all his helpers—those who follow his treatment plan—
   as long as they don't return to foolishly breaking his design for life.
9 His eternal restoration is most certainly available to all who honor him,
   that his glorious character of love may fill our land.
10 Love and truth are perfectly united;
   righteousness and peaceful wellness are inseparably entwined.
11 Truth will arise out of the earth,
   and righteousness smiles down from heaven.
12 The Lord will most certainly provide the remedy to restore goodness,
   and the earth will bring forth a harvest of the healed.
13 Righteousness will emanate from him
   and be the foundation of his life. ೞ

PSALM 86

A PRAYER OF DAVID

1 Pay special attention to me, O Lord, and please answer me,
    for I am frail, dying in my terminal state and need your help.
2 Save me from death, for I trust you with my life.
    Heal me, my Creator God, for I serve and trust only you.
3 Pour your healing remedy into my heart, O Lord,
    for my mind is in open communion with you all day long.
4 Give me the happiness that comes from healthiness of soul,
    because I have turned to you for renewal, Lord.
5 For you, Lord, are kind and forgiving,
    eager to pour your healing love into all who call on you.
6 Lord, pay special attention to my prayer;
    listen kindly to my cry for deliverance.
7 Whenever I am in trouble I call on you,
    for you always answer me.
8 Lord, there is no god like you among the pagan gods—
    none who creates and sustains life upon love like you do.
9 All the nations you have established
    will come and acknowledge you as worthy, Lord,
    and will honor your character of love.
10 For you are great and do amazing things;
    you alone are our Creator God.
11 Teach me how you built life to operate, O God,
    and I will live in harmony with your design;
    renew my heart into perfect adoration of your character of love.
12 I will praise you with my renewed heart, O Lord my God,
    and magnify your character of love forever.
13 For the outflow of your healing love to me is great:
    you cure my inmost being,
    delivering my individuality from deep torment and total disintegration.
14 O God, selfish and arrogant people rise up against me;
    a heartless gang seeks to kill me:
    they do not respect you or value your method of love.
15 But you, O Lord, are a compassionate, patient and gracious God—

the source of life-giving love and truth.
16 Come to me and pour your gracious remedy upon me;
    infuse your mighty transforming power into me
    and cure me, because I choose to serve you—just as my mother did.
17 Make me a sign of your goodness,
    that my enemies might see your healing in me and be ashamed,
    because you, O Lord, have renewed and restored me. ❧

Psalm 87

Life Is Found Only In You

1 The Lord founded his plan of salvation
    in the hills set apart for his sanctuary.
2 He loves the gates that lead to the restoration and healing of his children
    more than any other place in the world.
3 Glorious things are told about you,
    O city of our Creator God:
4 "I will include Egypt and Babylon among those who know me;
    also people from Philistia, Tyre and Ethiopia
    have been reborn to become citizens of Zion."
5 Of the New Jerusalem it will be said,
    "These were reborn to become her citizens,"
    and the Creator God himself will establish her.
6 The Lord will record the individualities of the saved
    in his heavenly registry, noting,
    "This one was reborn to live there."
7 Songs from those who are reborn will say,
    "Life is found only in you." ❧

Psalm 88

O Lord God, you are my Savior

1. O Lord God, you are my Savior;
     it is to you that I cry out—day and night.
2. May my prayer touch your heart—
     listen tenderly to my plea,
3. for my troubles overwhelm me;
     I feel like I'm about to die.
4. To my friends I'm useless, like one already dead—
     I'm so weak and worn out.
5. I'm abandoned among the lifeless;
     I feel like those already in the grave,
   like one you have forgotten—
     whose life is beyond your care.
6. You have let me sink so deep that I am close to death;
     I am in the darkest pits of despair.
7. I feel like you are angry with me;
     I am drowning in waves of discouragement.
8. My friends have abandoned me—
     they find me repulsive;
     I feel trapped with no way out.
9. My eyes are swollen from crying.
     Lord, to you I cry out all day long;
     I reach out my hands to you.
10. Do you perform wonders to reach the dead?
      Do they stand up and give you praise?
11. Do those in the grave live out your love?
      Do the dead respond to your faithfulness?
12. Is your perfect design for life celebrated in the darkest grave
      or your righteous character of love in the land where nothing lives?
13. But I call to you for help, O Lord;
      each morning my prayer greets you.
14. Lord, why do I feel abandoned?
      Why do I feel like you're hidden from me?
15. Ever since my youth—when I gave my heart to you—

I have been in conflict and have nearly died.
In your cause I have suffered many horrors and have been confused—
16   it seems like you want me overwhelmed,
          terrified and destroyed.
17   For all day long enemies surround me like a flood;
          they close in on me from every side.
18   All my friends and family have abandoned me;
          darkness is my only comfort. ∼

PSALM 89
THE HEAVENS REVEAL THE WONDERS OF YOUR DESIGN

1   I will sing of your character of love forever;
          I will proclaim your constancy and trustworthiness to all generations.
2   For I have said, "Your everlasting love is what life is built upon;
          your faithfulness is established in the skies above."
3   The Lord said, "I have made an agreement with the man I have chosen;
          I have promised my servant David:
4   'A descendant of yours will be King forever
          and through him your dynasty will never end.'"
5   Lord, the heavens reveal the wonders of your design;
          your faithful sustaining of all reality
          is also seen in the lives of all holy beings.
6   For who in the universe can compare with the Lord?
          Who among the heavenly beings is like our Creator God?
7   God is supremely honored and revered
          in the assembly of heaven's sinless beings,
          more awesome than all who surround him.
8   Lord God, Creator of all,
          Who has the ability to create and sustain reality like you?
          Your life-giving love and goodness constantly flow from you.
9   You reign over the majestic sea;
          when the waves rage, it is your presence that calms them.
10   Your power of truth and love has crushed the self-exalted one—

    the proud sea serpent;
    by the One who is your powerful Right Hand you defeat your enemies.
11 The heavens are yours and the earth is also yours;
    you built the world and everything in it.
12 Dimensions like north and south—you created them.
    Mount Tabor and Mount Hermon—teeming with life—
    give song to your character of love.
13 You have a Mighty One at your right arm;
    your hand is powerful;
    your right-hand Man is victorious in truth and love.
14 Your government is founded upon design-law—
    constants that are right and fair;
    life is sustained by other-centered love
    and infinite truth that emanates from you.
15 Happy and healthy are the people who celebrate your character of love;
    O Lord, they live in harmony with you,
    radiating the light of your presence.
16 They rejoice in your character and methods of love all day long
    and are transformed and exalted by your righteousness.
17 Your beautiful character of love is their remedy;
    in your love you give us the victory.
18 For the Lord is our protector,
    the Holy One of Israel is our King.
19 Long ago you spoke in a vision to your faithful spokesman
    and said, "I have given help to a famous warrior;
    I have chosen one from the common people to be king.
20 I have found David—he worships and serves me;
    with my holy oil I have anointed him king.
21 I will always be near him to help him,
    and my power will give him strength.
22 No enemy will ever enslave him;
    no wicked person will ever control him.
23 I will defeat his enemies
    and overthrow those who hate him.
24 My unfailing truth and eternal love will be with him,

and through my character and methods of love he will prevail.
²⁵ I will establish him as sovereign over a sea of people;
 he will govern over rivers of change.
²⁶ He will call out to me, 'You are my Father,
 my God, my rock-solid Remedy—my Savior.'
²⁷ I will designate him as my firstborn—the head of the royal line,
 the one whose heart has grown closest to mine
 of all the kings of the earth.
²⁸ I will maintain my loving plan for him forever,
 and my promise to him will never fail.
²⁹ I will establish his descendant forever;
 his throne will endure as long as the heavens last.
³⁰ But if his descendants reject my methods
 and do not live in harmony with my design for life,
³¹ if they refuse to follow my treatment plan
 and do not obey the laws that I have created life to operate upon,
³² I will intervene therapeutically with a shepherd's rod
 and diagnose them as stricken with sin and sick.
³³ I will never abort my loving plan for him
 nor break my promise to him.
³⁴ I will not violate my pledge to him
 or change what I said I would do.
³⁵ One oath I have sworn by my holiness
 (and I will not lie to David):
³⁶ His descendant will reign forever,
 his throne will be a radiant sun of righteousness in my presence—
³⁷ everlasting like the moon—
 a perpetual evidence of goodness for all to see."
³⁸ But, you, O God, must have rejected him;
 you must have turned away from your chosen king.
³⁹ You must have abandoned your pledge to him;
 surely you are going to give his crown to another,
⁴⁰ for you have permitted his defenses to be overrun
 and his strongholds to be demolished.
⁴¹ All who come by rob him;

he is mocked by his neighbors.
⁴² Surely you have strengthened his enemies
and his adversaries now celebrate their victory.
⁴³ You have made his sword useless,
for you have not stood beside him in battle.
⁴⁴ Because of all of this, you have brought to an end his majesty
and ground his royal reputation in the dirt.
⁴⁵ You have made him old before his time
and covered him with disgrace.
⁴⁶ How long, O Lord, will this go on? Will you remain hidden forever?
When we reject your methods and you let us go,
it seems like the angriest fire.
⁴⁷ Remember how short human life is,
although you didn't create human beings to die.
⁴⁸ Yet, what human can live and never die?
Who can overcome the power of death?
⁴⁹ Lord, where are you?
Where are your interventions of love, like in times past—
the promises you told David you would faithfully fulfill?
⁵⁰ Lord, remember how your helpers are mocked,
how my heart is burdened by the insults of the selfish.
⁵¹ Lord, remember how the enemies of love have ridiculed you
and how they have ridiculed your anointed king.
⁵² Praise be to the Lord forever!
So let it always be. ❧

PSALM 90
YOUR WRATH TO DESTROY SIN IS AWE-INSPIRING

1   O Lord, you have always been our sanctuary—our oasis and safe haven—
        for every generation.

2   Before time began and the mountains were born,
            before you gave of yourself to give birth to the earth,
            from eternity past to eternity future, you are the Creator God.

3   In mercy—to limit the suffering from sin—you return human beings to dust,
            saying, "Return to dust, you offspring of Adam."

4   But this is but a brief respite in your healing plan:
            for you, a thousand years are like a single day—
            more like a few hours of the night.

5   In mercy, you permit us to fall asleep in death.
            We sprout like the flowers in the field—

6   in the morning we blossom bright and fresh,
            but by evening we wither and die.

7   Our sin-sickness comes to an end in your presence,
            therefore it terrifies us to be abandoned by you.

8   Our terminal condition is laid out before you,
            the corruption most deeply hidden in our souls is exposed in your presence.

9   All of our days we struggle to turn away from the selfishness which you hate;
            our lives end in mournful meditation.

10 We live for seventy years,
            or eighty years if we are strong;
        but our selfishness causes life to be hard—a struggle filled with sorrow;
            time flies by so quickly and we pass away.

11 Who really knows how angry it makes you that this happened to us?
            Your wrath to destroy sin is awe-inspiring.

12 Help us understand our terminal condition—how short life really is—
            so that we may have the wisdom to partake of your remedy
            and experience renewed hearts.

13 When will you turn to us, O Lord—
            turn and comfort your helpers?

14 Fill us each morning with your life-giving love,
            that our lives may be a joyful song

revealing your methods and character of love.
15 Make our joy last longer than our suffering—
    many years longer than we have struggled against evil.
16 Let your healing work be seen by your helpers
    and your glorious character of love by their children.
17 Let the beauty of the Lord our God be upon us
    and be the basis of the practices of our lives—
    even the works of our hands! ❧

PSALM 91
HE IS MY REMEDY AND MY SECURITY

1 All who live with renewed hearts—
    covered in the righteousness of the Most High—
    will rest under the protection of the Ruler of the universe.
2 They will say of the Lord, "He is my remedy and my security,
    my God, in whom I trust."
3 He will save you from devious traps—
    the pestilence of malicious speech and deadly lies.
4 He will cover you in his perfect righteousness,
    and under his healing care you will be renewed;
    his faithfulness will be your remedy and immunity.
5 You will not be afraid of the dreadful fears that assail the mind in the dark,
    nor the verbal attacks that fly like arrows in the daytime,
6 nor the pestilence of fear and doubt that creep into the heart at night,
    nor the plague of guilt and shame
    that destroys the soul when the light shines in.
7 A thousand may die of unremedied sin beside you
    and tens of thousands at your right hand,
    but eternal death will not come near you.
8 Yes, you will see with your own eyes
    how sin destroys those who reject my healing remedy.
9 Because you have made the Lord your shelter—

the Most High your abiding place—

10 no evil will infect your heart
   nor will corruption come into your home.

11 For he will command his angels to watch over you,
   to guard and protect you and keep you safe:

12 they will hold you in their hands,
   so that you won't hurt your foot stumbling on a stone.

13 You will tread upon evil forces—the ravenous lions and slithering snakes;
   you will trample the great lion—the predator of good, the ancient serpent.

14 The Lord says, "I will heal those who love and trust me;
   I will protect them because they have partaken of my character.

15 When they call out to me, I will answer them;
   I will be with them in times of trouble,
   I will rescue them from sinfulness
   and restore them to my glorious design.

16 I will heal them
   and give them eternal life." ଔ

PSALM 92

HOW MAGNIFICENT ARE ALL YOUR WORKS, O LORD

1   It is good to give thanks to the Lord
    and sing praises to your character of love, O Creator God,

2   to live out your love in the morning
    and your never-changing truth in the evening;

3   to have hearts in perfect harmony with you, like the music of the strings
    and the melody of the harp.

4   All your works, O Lord, fill me with happiness;
    I sing for joy at the universe you have created.

5   How magnificent are all your works, O Lord,
    how infinite are your thoughts!

6   Wicked and brutal people do not know,
    the foolish do not realize,

7   that though the selfish may spring up like grass
    and evildoers may attain fame and fortune—
    having rejected the remedy and embraced selfishness, they will die eternally.

8   But you, O Creator God,
    will be exalted in the hearts of the righteous forever.

9   Unavoidably, your enemies, O Lord,
    unavoidably, your enemies—those who oppose truth and love—will perish;
    all the persistently selfish will be severed from you, the source of life.

10 You have given me life and strength like that of a wild ox;
    the pure oil of your Spirit you have poured upon me.

11 I see clearly the terminal condition of those who oppose me;
    I understand the selfish motives of those who rise up against me.

12 Those with hearts healed to love will flourish like a palm tree,
    they will grow mighty in godliness like the cedars of Lebanon;

13 rooted in God's kingdom of love and truth,
    they will live in the dwelling place of our God.

14 Though old, they stay healthy and bear much fruit;
    they retain their vitality and remain vibrant,

15 proclaiming, "The Lord is perfect and righteous;
    he is my source of life, health and happiness,
    and there is nothing evil in him." ◌

Psalm 93

The Lord Reigns Supreme, Covered in Majesty of Love

¹ The Lord reigns supreme, covered in majesty;
    the Lord is covered in majesty—the majesty of infinite love
    secured and bound by the strength of infinite truth.
  The world is established as the showcase of your methods of love;
    your design-laws for life cannot be changed.
² Your rulership was established long ago when you built all reality;
    you created time and existed before time began.
³ Seas of selfish beings have risen up, O Lord,
    the seas of the selfish have raised their voices in opposition to your rule;
    the seas of the selfish have pounded against your kingdom of truth and love.
⁴ Love is mightier than the thundering flood of selfishness;
    truth is mightier than the stormy seas of lies and deceit—
    the Lord, Creator God on high, is mighty!
⁵ Your design protocols for life can never be changed;
    holiness and healthiness—perfection in all things—adorn your house
    for all eternity, O Lord. ❧

Psalm 94

In union with my God is where I find safety

1. O Lord, the God who exterminates evil!
   O God, eradicate fear and selfishness—
   let your love and truth shine forth.
2. Rise up, O Creator who governs the earth;
   let the proud reap what they have sown.
3. How long, O Lord, will your mercy shield the wicked?
   How long will they celebrate in their terminal state?
4. They are constant torrent of self-importance;
   the selfish overflow with boasting.
5. They walk all over your people, O Lord;
   they oppress those who have your character of love.
6. They kill the powerless, widows and immigrants
   and murder the orphans—those without family.
7. They tell themselves, "The Lord does not see;
   the God whom Jacob worshipped doesn't even know."
8. But know this, you who deny reality and live in ignorance;
   you foolish people, when will you wise up?
9. God created our ears—don't you realize he hears everything?
   God created our eyes—don't you realize he sees everything?
10. The Lord disciplines the nations, so get this straight:
    he will reveal the truth to correct the people
    and teach them how reality works!
11. The Lord knows how the worldly-wise think;
    he knows that their selfish ideas are misleading, destructive and futile.
12. Happy and healthy is the person whom you disciple, O Lord—
    the person you teach to live in harmony with your design-law for life;
13. you provide them healing and deliverance from the day of trouble,
    but the wicked dig the pit of their own eternal destruction.
14. The Lord will not abandon his people—those who partake of the remedy;
    he will never forsake his inheritance—
    those who possess his character of love.
15. Justice returns to design-law—the law upon which life is built to operate;
    and all the healed—those who are pure in heart—live in harmony with it.

¹⁶ Who will help me fight against selfishness?
  Who will stand with me against those who promote evil?
¹⁷ If the Lord had not given me his remedy,
  I would have quickly succumbed to the silence of death.
¹⁸ When I said, "I am slipping into selfishness,"
  your perfect love, O Lord, healed me.
¹⁹ When doubts and fears trouble my mind,
  abiding in your truth and love brings peace to my soul.
²⁰ Selfish leaders who practice evil are not allied with you;
  they pass imposed laws to cause suffering and injustice.
²¹ They plot together against the pure of heart
  and condemn the innocent to death.
²² But the Lord protects me;
  in union with my God is where I find safety.
²³ The Lord will allow the wicked to reap what they have sown;
  their rejection of the remedy and persistent wickedness destroys them,
  and the Lord will sadly let them go. ♁

PSALM 95

HE GOVERNS AND SUSTAINS ALL REALITY

1 O Come, let us sing together for joy to the Lord;
   let us shout to God our Remedy who heals us, how glad we are.

2 Come into his presence with thankful hearts
   and let our lives be songs of love celebrating him.

3 For the Lord is the great Creator God,
   the Supreme Ruler—the source of life—above all gods.

4 He governs and sustains all reality,
   from the earth's core to the highest mountains.

5 The sea is his, for he made it,
   and he created the dry land.

6 Come, let us bow down in humble worship;
   let us kneel before our Maker,

7 for he is our Creator God
   and we are the people he is treating—
   the flock of wounded under his care.
   Today, if you hear his voice
   offering healing and restoration,

8 do not reject the true remedy and harden your hearts
   as you did in Meribah,
   as you did in the rebellion in the desert at Massah,
   during the opportunity to take God's cure,

9 where your fathers broke my heart
   by trying their own remedies
   and rejected the healing truth I brought.

10 For forty years I patiently tried to heal them
   and was angry that they wouldn't let me;
   I said, "These people prefer selfishness; they refuse my remedy
   and will not embrace my design-laws for life."

11 Angry that they wouldn't let me heal them, I declared the reality:
   "Since they refuse the remedy I freely offer,
   they will never be able to enter my rest and get well." ❧

Psalm 96

His design laws apply equally to everyone

1 Sing to the Lord a new heart-song;
     sing to the Lord, all the earth!
2 Sing to the Lord, praise his character of love;
     display his healing and restoration in you each and every day.
3 Take the truth of his glorious character and methods of love
       to the entire world,
     tell everyone of his marvelous works,
4 for supreme is the Lord and most worthy of adoration:
     he is to be awed, admired, and esteemed above all gods.
5 For every god of this world is a worthless fraud,
     but the Lord is the Creator who made the heavens.
6 Majestic love and splendid truth emanate from him;
     power and glory fill his dwelling place.
7 Recognize the Lord, all peoples of the world;
     recognize the Lord as glorious and almighty!
8 Give your Creator the adoration his character of love deserves;
     bring yourselves into his presence,
     offering your love and devotion.
9 Worship the Lord with your hearts renewed with the beauty of his holiness;
     abide in his presence all the earth!
10 Say to the nations, "The Creator built reality, and he sustains and rules over it."
     The world is firmly established on universal laws that cannot be changed;
     his design-laws apply equally to everyone.
11 Let the earth and sky rejoice;
     let the oceans roar in victory, and everything within them.
12 Let the fields with their lavish crops celebrate
     and all the trees in the forests exclaim with joy;
13 they will sing before the Lord, for he is coming—
     he is coming to govern the earth!
   He will govern the world, restoring it back to his perfect design,
     and the people will live in truth—in harmony with his character of love. ◌

PSALM 97

THE FIRES OF TRUTH AND LOVE FLOW FROM HIM

1   The Creator reigns in love; let the earth rejoice!
        Let every distant land celebrate his constant care.
2   His infinite depths are like impenetrable clouds surrounding him;
        He rules in righteousness, governing in love.
3   The fires of truth and love flow from him like mighty rivers;
        they completely consume selfishness and falsehood—his fierce enemies.
4   Truth and love flash forth from him and light up the world;
        the earthly see it and tremble.
5   The high-places of false worship melt like wax in his presence—
        in the presence of the Creator of all the earth.
6   The heavens proclaim his design and methods of love,
        and all the peoples of the earth see his glorious character of love.
7   All worshippers of idols damage their hearts and minds—
        all those who make the created things their god.
    The fallen angels—the inventors of the false gods—
        will bow down before him.
8   God's people hear the truth and rejoice;
        all who trust you, Lord, are glad,
        for your remedy heals perfectly those who put their trust in you.
9   For you, O Lord, are the Creator and Sustainer of the earth;
        you are supreme, and your existence is far above all other so-called gods.
10 Those who love the Lord hate evil:
        the Lord heals the souls of those who trust him
        and delivers them from the power of the selfish.
11 The light of truth and love shines upon the righteous;
        joy fills those who are right-in-heart with God.
12 Rejoice in the Lord, all you whose hearts are united with God,
        and praise his character of love. ❧

PSALM 98

THE LORD HAS REVEALED HIS PERFECT DESIGN FOR LIFE

1 Sing a new heart-song to the Lord,
> for what he has done is astounding:
Jesus—his Right Hand and Holy Agent—
> is the cure for sin.
2 The Lord has made his Remedy known
> and revealed his perfect and right design for life to the nations.
3 He has kept his promise
> to pour out his love and truth upon his people;
the entire world has seen
> the healing power of our God.
4 Let everyone make their life a joyful song unto the Lord!
> Let the beautiful music of love burst forth from your hearts renewed;
5 make the melody of love for the Lord, resplendent like the sound of the harp;
> let your love resound with the harp and singing.
6 With trumpets and horns,
> proclaim your joy for the Lord our King.
7 Let the sea and everything dwelling in it rejoice
> along with the entire world and all who inhabit it.
8 Let the rivers celebrate
> and the mountains shout for joy;
9 let them sing to the Lord,
> for he comes to restore his governance to the earth.
He will govern the world in love
> and heal the people to live in harmony with his design for life. ⌀

Psalm 99

The Lord reigns in love and truth

1   The Lord reigns in love and truth—
        let the selfish world tremble!
    He sits enthroned above the winged angels—
        let all the selfish people be shaken.
2   The Lord is great in Zion;
        he is supreme over all people.
3   Let everyone praise your great and awesome character of love, O God,
        which is perfection and holiness.
4   Mighty King, you love healing your creation—putting things right;
        you have established life to operate upon your design of love.
    What you have done in Israel, revealing your remedy,
        is completely right and just.
5   Praise the Lord our Creator;
        bow down in worship before his throne,
        for he is perfection and holiness.
6   Moses and Aaron were his priests—his helpers to share the remedy,
        Samuel called for the Lord to reveal his character;
    they called for the Lord to act
        and he answered them.
7   He spoke his plan to them from the pillar of cloud;
        they followed his directions and trusted his prescription.
8   O Lord our Creator,
        you answered them;
    you were a forgiving God to your people,
        working with them to purge all deviations from your design for life.
9   Praise the Lord our Creator
        and worship at his holy mountain,
        for the Lord is perfection and holiness. ❧

Psalm 100

He is love beautiful and everlasting

1 Shout the victory of the Lord, all the earth!
2 Be eager and glad to fulfill God's calling,
    and you will enter his presence with songs of joy.
3 Know that the Lord is our Creator God;
    it is he who made us and we are his:
    we are his children—the people he loves, nourishes and protects.
4 Enter his gates with thankful hearts
    and his courts with praise;
    give him your thanks, and praise his glorious character of love.
5 For the Lord is good; he is love beautiful and everlasting;
    he is always true—for all time, through every generation. ◌

Psalm 101

I will sing of your kingdom of love

1   I will sing of your kingdom of love;
        my life will be a song praising your character of love, O Lord.
2   Understanding your design-laws, I will live in harmony with them—
        how long until you restore me to perfect unity with you?
    In my house, I will live out your law of love
        with a pure heart.
3   I will not cherish selfishness—anything vile or wicked;
        I hate all actions which deviate from your design,
        and such corruption will not be part of my character.
4   Selfish temptations shall be purged completely from my heart;
        no evil will be permitted to attach to me.
5   I will terminate my relationship
        with anyone who slanders others;
    I will cut out of my life
        those who cling to pride and arrogance.
6   I will seek out those in the world who love you and are loyal to you,
        and I will make them my friends;
        those who are pure in heart will carry out my purposes.
7   Deceivers will not live in my house;
        the dishonest will not remain in my presence.
8   Every day I work to eliminate wickedness,
        to purify and cleanse the world,
    that I may cut out all deviations from God's design
        and restore the city of the Lord to perfection. ↭

Psalm 102

You Pour Out Your Healing Love Upon Your People

1 O Lord, please listen to me when I call out to you;
    hear my cry for help.
2 In my distress, it feels like you have abandoned me;
    please don't neglect me.
    Move close to me and pay special attention;
    when I call, please come quickly.
3 For my life is fading away like smoke;
    my bones are brittle, worn, and charred like coals in a fire.
4 My heart is torn, and I am withering away like grass;
    I am so distraught I forget to eat.
5 Because of my grief
    I am wasting away—just skin and bones.
6 I am like a pelican lost in the desert,
    a solitary owl lost in the wastelands.
7 I cannot sleep;
    I am alone in the night like a bird on a roof.
8 All day long my enemies mock me;
    the selfish and arrogant swear against me.
9 My food tastes like ash,
    and my drink is mixed with tears.
10 Because of your anger at sin and the destruction it causes,
    you have surrendered me to be the cure and then exalted me. [7]
11 My life is coming to an end like the evening shadow;
    I am withering away like grass.
12 But you, O Creator God, are the eternal source and sustainer of life;
    your character and methods of love endure forever.
13 You shall arise and pour out your healing love upon your people,
    for the time to provide your gracious remedy has come;
    the appointed time has arrived.
14 Those who serve you will cherish your living stones
    and show mercy to their descendants.
15 People from all nations will revere and admire the Lord,

---

[7] This is interpreted as a Messianic Psalm referring to Christ's experience at Gethsemane and the Cross.

and leaders from around the world will honor your character of love.
16 For the Lord will recreate the earth in perfection
    and appear in his unveiled glory.
17 He will gently turn and answer the plea of those who acknowledge their need;
    he will not reject their request for renewal of heart.
18 His healing interventions will be recorded for future generations,
    that a renewed and recreated people may praise the Lord.
19 The Lord looked down from his heavenly sanctuary;
    from heaven the Lord examined the earth,
20 to hear the groans of those held captive in sin and selfishness
    and free them from their terminal condition,
21 so that God's character of love will be revealed throughout the earth
    and praised in the New Jerusalem
22 when the people of God assemble to worship the Lord
    and the nations serve him.
23 He placed on me the affliction,
    crushing my strength and cutting my life short:
24 I cried out to him,
    "If it be possible, take this cup from me and don't let me die in midlife, O God—
    you who are eternal and live forever, through all generations!"
25 In the beginning, O Son, you created the earth;
    the sun, moon and planets of this solar system are a work of your hands.
26 They will be destroyed, but you will live forever;
    they will all wear out like old clothing;
you will roll them up like a coat—
    like old garments they will be changed for new.
27 But you never change:
    you remain the same forever, and your years will never end.
28 The children of those who love and serve you will live in your presence;
    their descendants will be transformed to be like you. ෬

PSALM 103

HE RESTORES HIS CREATION TO HARMONY WITH HIS DESIGN

1 Praise the Lord, O my soul;
   with all that is within me, praise his perfect character of love!
2 Praise the Lord, O my soul,
   and do not forget all he does to heal us:
3 He forgives all our deviations from his design-law for life
   and provides the remedy to our sin-sickness,
4 delivering us from eternal death
   and enveloping us in his love and tender mercies;
5 he fills and adorns us with his goodness
   and gives us new life—a rebirth—to soar free like an eagle.
6 The Lord does what is right—
   he restores his creation to harmony with his design,
   healing those who are crushed by sin and selfishness.
7 He made known his ways to Moses,
   his methods to the people of Israel:
8 The Lord is merciful and gracious;
   he is infinite in love, holding on as long as there is hope—
9 yet he will not strive for all eternity to win our hearts;
   he will not hold back forever letting us go our own rebellious way.
10 He doesn't lay on us what our terminal sin-condition rightly deserves
   or leave us to rot in character, as our selfishness would naturally do.
11 As high as heaven is above the earth,
   so mighty is his love to heal those who revere him;
12 as far as the east is from the west,
   so far he removes the infection of fear and selfishness from us.
13 As a father tenderly pours love upon his children,
   so the Lord tenderly pours his love upon those who revere him;
14 for he knows how we are made,
   and he realizes we are descended from one man who was formed from mud.
15 For human life is like grass:
   we blossom like flowers in the field,
16 then the winds of time blow and the flower is gone,
   and where it grew no one remembers.
17 But from eternity past to eternity future,

the love of the Lord flows out to those who revere him—
    his righteous remedy healing all generations
18 who participate in his treatment plan
    and live in harmony with his design protocols for life.
19 The Creator God has established his throne in heaven,
    and his kingdom of love governs over all creation.
20 Praise the Lord, you loyal angels of God—
    you mighty beings who do his bidding,
    who carry out his commands.
21 Praise the Lord, all who live in heaven—
    you who live devoted to doing his will.
22 Praise the Lord, everything he has created,
    throughout his entire domain.
Praise the Lord, O my soul. ⍹

PSALM 104

YOUR GREATNESS IS BEYOND MEASURE

1 Praise the Lord, O my soul.
    O Lord my Creator God, your greatness is beyond measure;
you are clothed in the brilliance of infinite truth
    and the majesty of pure love.
2 You wear light like a robe;
    you have spread out the heavens like a starry curtain
3 and built the upper stratosphere out of water.[8]
    You make the clouds your chariot
    and travel throughout space and time via your Spirit.[9]
4 You make angels your messengers,
    your servants—fiery channels of heavenly light.
5 You established the earth in its orbit;
    it will never be removed.

---

[8] Genesis 1:7

[9] The Hebrew for "wings" כָּנָף הָ־ אָרֶץ [kā·nāp̄ hă-'ĕ·rĕṣ] is [also interpreted as "very distant place, formally, ends of the earth" [Swanson, J. (1997). Dictionary of Biblical Languages with Semantic Domains: Hebrew (Old Testament)] and the Hebrew for "wind" רוּחַ [ruwach /roo·akh/] is also interpreted as spirit.

6   You covered it with deep water like a garment;
           the waters stood above the mountains.
7   At your command the waters withdrew;
           when your voice thundered, the waters fled—
8   they flowed over the rising mountains and through the valleys
           to the places you prepared for them.
9   You set a boundary the waters cannot cross;
           never again will they cover the entire earth.
10   You made springs to flow down valleys,
           forming rivers to course through the hills.
11   They provide water for all the animals,
           the wild donkeys drink their fill.
12   The birds make their nests by the streams
           and sing their songs among the branches of the trees.
13   You send rain from above to water the hills;
           the earth is filled with the fruit you cause to grow.
14   You make the grass grow to feed the cattle,
           and crops for people to cultivate
           and produce food from the earth,
15   wine for people to celebrate,
           olive oil to give vitality,
           and food that sustains health.
16   The trees of the Lord have plenty of water—
           the cedars of Lebanon that he planted;
17   the birds nest in their branches,
           the heron makes its home in the evergreens.
18   Wild goats live in the high mountains
           and badgers make their home in the rocks.
19   You made the moon to mark the months,
           and the sun knows when to set.
20   You made the night, and in the darkness
           the wild animals of the forest roam about.
21   The lions roar for their prey
           but seek their food from God;
22   when the sun rises, they withdraw
           and return to their dens to rest.

23 Then people go out to their work
    and labor until evening.
24 O Lord, how incredible is the number of living things you have made!
    With your wisdom you fashioned them all;
    the earth is filled with your creatures.
25 The vast and spacious ocean
    is teeming with creatures too numerous to count—
    living things both large and small;
26 on its surface, ships sail to and fro,
    and the whale you created frolics in it.
27 All of your creatures depend upon you
    to provide them with food when they need it.
28 When you supply their food,
    they gather it in;
when you open your hand to feed them,
    they are filled with good things.
29 When your presence is hidden,
    they are afraid;
when your life-giving presence—the breath of life—is withdrawn,
    they die and return to dust.
30 When your Spirit returns, bringing the breath of life,
    creation happens and your creatures live,
    and the face of the earth is renewed.
31 May the glorious character of our Creator God endure forever;
    may the Lord find joy and love in his creatures.
32 He looks at the earth and it trembles;
    when he touches the mountains, they smoke.
33 I will sing praises to the Lord as long as I live;
    I will worship my Creator God of love for all of my days.
34 May all of my thoughts be pleasing to him,
    for I will rejoice in the Lord.
35 May all selfishness and every deviation from God's design
    vanish from the earth and wickedness be no more.
Praise the Lord, O my soul;
    Praise the Lord! C3

PSALM 105

HIS DESIGN-LAWS GOVERN THE ENTIRE EARTH

1 Give thanks to the Lord, proclaim his character of love;
   teach the people throughout the world
   his methods of love built right into nature.
2 Sing to him, sing of his wonderful ways,
   tell of all his incredible acts.
3 Boast of his perfection—his character of infinite love and truth,
   for the hearts of those who seek the Lord will rejoice.
4 Seek the Lord and the strength of character he gives;
   seek his presence continually.
5 Remember the surpassing excellence
   of what he has created,
   the miracles he has performed,
   and the perfection of his pronouncements.
6 You, who are like his servant Abraham in character,
   you chosen ones, who overcome with God, like Israel did:
7 he is the Lord our God,
   his design-laws govern the entire earth.
8 He will honor the agreement he made—
   the promise he spoke to show mercy to a thousand generations—
9 the covenant he made with Abraham;
   the vow he affirmed to Isaac—
10 the promised Messiah he reaffirmed to Jacob as a decree,[10]
   to Israel as an everlasting vow:
11 "To you I will give the land of Canaan
   as a pledge to your heritage."
12 When they were few in number—
   a tiny group of strangers in the land—
13 they moved from one nation to another,
   from one kingdom to the next.
14 He let no one oppress them
   and rebuked kings for their sake:
15 "Do not touch my chosen ones;

---

10 Genesis 28:14, 49:10.

       do not harm my spokespersons."

16 He foretold the famine to come upon the land
     and the destruction of all their food;

17 and he sent a man ahead of them—
     Joseph—sold as a slave.

18 They wounded his feet with shackles
     and put an iron collar around his neck,

19 until what he predicted came to pass
     and the word of the Lord proved him right.

20 The king of Egypt sent for him and set him free—
     the ruler of the nation released him.

21 He made Joseph ruler of his palace
     and governor over the nation,

22 with authority to bind
     all other princes and leaders to his will
     and teach the senior staff his wisdom.

23 Then Israel moved to Egypt;
     Jacob lived as a guest in the land of Ham.

24 The Lord blessed his helpers and they multiplied greatly;
     they became too numerous for their enemies,

25 whose hearts became fearful and they hated his helpers;
     they plotted against his spokespeople.

26 He sent Moses—his spokesman—
     and Aaron, whom he had chosen.

27 They revealed God's power,
     showing miraculous signs among them—
the evidence in the land of Ham
     that Yahweh is the true God.

28 He showed that their sun-god was false
     by sending darkness upon the land—
for not all the people were beyond reach,
     not all persisted in rebelling against the truth.

29 He showed that the Nile god was false
     by turning their water into blood,
     causing the fish to die.

30 Their land was overrun with frogs,
    even invading the bedrooms of their kings.
31 He spoke, and flies swarmed the land,
    and gnats invaded their nation.
32 He sent them hail instead of rain,
    and fierce lightning fell throughout their countryside;
33 their grapevines and fig trees were destroyed,
    and all the great trees in their land were shattered.
34 He spoke, and locust appeared—
    swarms of uncountable locusts plundered the land;
35 they ate up everything green in their land,
    and all their crops were consumed.
36 He put the firstborn of their nation to sleep in the grave—
    the firstfruits of their procreative power.
37 Then he brought Israel out of Egypt, laden with silver and gold,
    and none of the people became exhausted or stumbled.
38 Egyptians were glad they had left,
    because they had become terrified of Israel.
39 God spread out a cloud to cover them during the day,
    and a pillar of fire to give them warmth and light at night.
40 They begged, so he brought them quail,
    but God provided manna—bread of heaven—
    to satisfy all their nutritional needs.
41 He opened a rock and water gushed out;
    it flowed like a river into the desert.
42 For he remembered his sacred promise
    given to his spokesman Abraham.
43 He brought his helpers out with rejoicing,
    the ones he chose as the avenue for the Messiah,
    with shouts of joy.
44 He gave them the lands of those who refused to help God,
    and they took possession of the labor of others,
45 so that they might follow God's prescription
    and live in harmony with his design-laws for life.
    Praise the Lord! ଔ

Psalm 106

You, O Lord, bring healing to your helpers

1 Praise the Lord!
  Pour forth your thanks to the Lord, for he is good;
    his perfect and life-giving love is everlasting.
2 Who can adequately reveal the Lord's infinite power of love and truth
    or fully declare his beautiful character of love?
3 Happy and healthy are those who live in harmony with God's design-laws,
    who continually do what is right.
4 Remember me, O Lord: when you bring healing to your helpers,
    bring your remedy also to me.
5 Let me see your chosen helpers transformed,
    that I may celebrate the joy of your people
    and boast of your glory with those who belong to you.
6 We have been selfish, even as our ancestors were;
    we have broken your design of love and acted wickedly.
7 Our ancestors in Egypt did not appreciate what your mighty miracles revealed;
    they did not remember your many acts of love,
    and at the Red Sea they rebelled against your love and chose selfishness.
8 Despite this, he delivered them, revealing his character of love
    and making known his mighty power to save.
9 He commanded the Red Sea, and it dried up;
    he led them through where deep waters once were,
    on ground as dry as desert.
10 He delivered them from the power of Satan (the one who hated them),
    and from their true enemy—fear and selfishness—he provided freedom.
11 The waters drowned their enemies;
    not one of them survived.
12 Then they believed his promises
    and sang praises to him,
13 but soon they forgot all he had done
    and no longer waited for his instructions.
14 In the desert they gave in to insatiable cravings
    and demanded that God prove himself.
15 So he gave them what they insisted upon,
    but it only brought sickness upon them.

16 In the camp the people became jealous of Moses and of Aaron—
    the holy priest of the Lord.
17 The earth split open and devoured Dathan;
    it covered over the group led by Abiram.
18 Fire burned through their followers;
    flames consumed the wicked.
19 At Sinai they made an image of a calf
    and worshiped an idol made out of metal.
20 They traded the glory of their infinite God
    for an image of a grass-eating bull.
21 They ignored and neglected the God who delivered them,
    who performed mighty miracles in Egypt,
22 wonderful things in the land of Ham
    and awesome acts by the Red Sea.
23 So he said he would destroy them,
    but Moses, his chosen helper, did exactly what God foreknew—
in love, he argued for the Lord's reputation,
    and the Lord did not let them go or be destroyed.
24 Then they refused to enter the rich and fruitful land;
    they did not believe his promise.
25 They stayed in their tents and complained
    and would not follow the treatment-plan of the Lord.
26 So he told them the unavoidable reality of what they had chosen:
    having rejected his healing plan, they would die in the desert,
27 and their descendants who reject his plan will die among the heathen,
    scattered throughout the nations.
28 They gave their hearts to Baal of Peor
    and ate sacrifices offered to the lifeless idols.
29 The Lord was angered by their self-destructive choices
    but let them go their own way, and a plague broke out among them.
30 But Phinehas took a stand and intervened to cut out the rebellious,
    and the plague was stopped.
31 His stand for God and rejection of Baal was recognized as right,
    and all succeeding generations will agree.
32 By the waters of Meribah they displeased the Lord,
    and Moses suffered because of them;

33 they irritated Moses and he spoke impulsively, without thinking.
34 They did not eradicate the incurable heathen peoples
     as the Lord instructed them
35 but joined and mixed with the pagan nations
     and learned to think and act like them.
36 They worshipped their false gods and their hearts were enslaved by fear—
     their minds were darkened and characters ruined.
37 They sacrificed their sons
     and their daughters to demons.
38 They shed the blood of the innocent—the blood of their own sons and daughters,
     whom they sacrificed to appease the idols of Canaan,
     until the entire country was corrupted by the belief in human sacrifice.
39 By what they did, they seared their consciences and corrupted their characters;
     they committed adultery by betraying God and giving their hearts to idols.
40 The Lord was angry that his helpers chose to destroy their souls;
     he was sickened watching his helpers degrade themselves.
41 He let them go their way and surrendered them to the heathen,
     and their enemies enslaved them.
42 Their foes were cruel to them
     and kept them under their power.
43 Many times the Lord delivered them,
     but their hearts were selfish, hardened in rebellion,
     and they wasted away, dying in their terminal sin-sick state.
44 But he saw how they suffered
     and heard their cry for help.
45 In mercy, he fulfilled his vow to them
     and out of his great love he intervened in their behalf;
46 he caused their captors
     to treat them with kindness.
47 Heal us, O Lord our Creator God, gather us from the selfish world,
     that we may give thanks to your perfection—your holy character of love—
     and glorify and praise your character in our lives.
48 Thanksgiving and adoration be to the Creator God of Israel
     for all eternity and evermore.
     Let all the people say, "So let it always be."
     Praise the Lord! ❧

PSALM 107
THOSE WHO THIRST FOR RIGHTEOUSNESS HE SATISFIES

1 Give thanks to the Creator God, for he is good;
   his law of love is unchanging and endures forever.
2 All whom the Lord has rescued will say this—
   all whom he has rescued from the power of the enemy,
3 whom he gathers from the earth—
   from east and west, from north and south.
4 Some wandered through the wilderness of this world—a desert devoid of love—
   finding no way to enter the city where they could obtain rest.
5 They were hungry and thirsty—in need of righteousness;
   their lives slowly ebbed away.
6 In distress they called to the Lord
   and he healed them of their terminal sin-condition.
7 He led them to live the right way—down the straight and narrow path—
   that they might walk the road of life to the city where they would live.
8 Oh, give thanks to the Lord for his unfailing love
   and his wonderful acts of love to heal humanity:
9 those who thirst for righteousness he satisfies,
   and those who hunger for good he fills.
10 Some sat in the darkness of lies and the deep gloom of hopelessness,
   prisoners of fear and selfishness, suffering in chains they could not break,
11 for they had rebelled against the designs of the Creator God
   and rejected healing plan of the Most High.
12 So he taught them by letting them have their way, and life became hard;
   they ruined themselves and there was no one to help.
13 They cried out to the Lord in their distress
   and he provided remedy for their terminal condition.
14 He brought them out of the darkness of lies and the gloom of hopelessness
   and broke the chains of fear and selfishness.
15 Oh, give thanks to the Lord for his unfailing love
   and his wonderful acts of love to heal humanity,
16 for he destroys death's door [11]

---

[11] Bronze is an impure metal (a mix of two—not pure gold or silver) and thus was symbolic of the 'carnal heart,' which is the way to death. Through Christ, God destroys this, thus he "destroyed death and brought life and immortality to light." 2Tim 1:10.

and severs every tie to sin.

17 Those who broke God's design-laws damaged their minds and became fools;
   they suffered because they broke the protocols of life.

18 Their appetites hated the food that would heal their souls
   and they were knocking on death's door.

19 They cried out to the Lord in their distress
   and he provided remedy for their terminal condition.

20 He sent forth his Word and healed them;
   he saved them from death.

21 Oh, give thanks to the Lord for his unfailing love
   and his wonderful acts of love to heal humanity.

22 Let them present offerings of thanksgiving
   and proclaim his methods of love with songs of joy.

23 Those who go out on the sea in ships,
   who carried cargo over the mighty waters,

24 have seen how the Lord works—
   his amazing ability to govern the deepest oceans.

25 For he speaks and causes the stormy winds to stand still—
   the winds that drive the waves to swell.

26 Rising high in the air and falling deep in the depths,
   the sailors became terrified.

27 They stumbled and staggered like a drunk
   and didn't know what else they could do.

28 They cried out to the Lord in their distress
   and he delivered them from certain death.

29 He caused the stormy winds to stand still,
   and the angry waves were calmed.

30 The sailors rejoiced because the waves calmed down,
   and he guided them to the safe haven they sought.

31 Oh, give thanks to the Lord for his unfailing love
   and his wonderful acts of love to save humanity.

32 Exalt him and his methods of love, wherever people assemble,
   and praise him before the leaders of nations.

33 He turned rivers into deserts,
   flowing springs into dry ground

³⁴ and changed fruitful land into salt
    to put an end to the wickedness happening there.
³⁵ He turned a desert into wetlands,
    dry ground into flowing springs,
³⁶ and the hungry settled there
    and established a city to live in.
³⁷ They sowed fields and planted vineyards
    that brought a fruitful harvest;
³⁸ he blessed them, and they increased in number
    and their livestock did not decrease.
³⁹ When they are diminished and degraded
    by wickedness, coercion and grief,
⁴⁰ he shows contempt on their arrogant leaders by letting them go,
    and their lives become aimless, empty wastes.
⁴¹ But he heals and uplifts out of misery those who recognize their need,
    increasing their families and causing them to prosper.
⁴² Those set right in heart with God understand and rejoice,
    but all who prefer selfishness have nothing to say.
⁴³ Those who are wise will learn from these things
    and understand how great the Lord's law of love truly is. ℘

PSALM 108
HIS TRUSTWORTHINESS SUSTAINS THE SKY

1 My heart is set right with you, O God;
   my life is a song glorifying your character of love.
2 Awake, my harp and all my instruments,
   to start each day with a song of love,
3 giving thanks to you before all peoples,
   giving praise to you before all nations.
4 For your love is great, overarching, permeating and governing the heavens;
   your trustworthiness sustains the sky.
5 Be exalted as Creator—God who built all the heavens—
   and let your glorious character of love shine over all the earth.
6 Heal and restore us with your power,
   that those who accept your love may be transformed.
7 God has spoken from his dwelling place:
   "I will rejoice to give humanity the earth—
   all of it, until east meets west.
8 Gilead in the east and Manasseh in the west are mine;
   Ephraim will be a strong leader,
   Judah will be the father of the Sovereign.
9 Enemies like Moab will be washed away,
   foes like Edom will be cast off like a worn-out shoe.
   Because of me, enemies like Philistia cry out."
10 Who will lead me into the fortified city?
   Who will lead me into Edom?
11 O God, you haven't given up on us, have you?
   Are you refusing to fight in our behalf?
12 O help us out of our affliction,
   for all our efforts to save ourselves are worthless.
13 In union with God we will be restored—strong and healthy,
   and he will defeat our enemy. ଔ

Psalm 109

The Lord diagnoses accurately

1 O God, I adore and praise you,
 do not remain silent,
2 for self-centered liars slander me;
 they say all manner of falsehood against me.
3 Everywhere I turn I hear their hateful words;
 they attack me for no reason.
4 I pour my love upon them but they resist it,
 yet I keep praying for them.
5 They misrepresent my good as evil
 and hate my love.
6 Place their wickedness back upon them;
 let all see it is Satan, the evil one, at their right hand who leads them.
7 When they are examined, they will be found incurable;
 their selfish prayers confirm their terminal condition.
8 Their lives will be cut short
 and others will take their place.
9 Their children will be orphans
 and their spouses widowed.
10 Their families wander aimlessly
 begging for handouts, evicted from their dilapidated homes.
11 Creditors seize their property;
 strangers take all they worked for.
12 They accept love from no one
 or mercy for their orphaned children.
13 Their descendants who cling to selfishness will die incurable,
 their corrupt characters purged from future generations.
14 The Lord diagnoses accurately the sin-sickness of their fathers;
 their mothers refused to allow sinfulness to be cut out of their hearts.
15 The Lord will always remember their choice for selfishness,
 but on earth they will be forgotten.
16 They never gave to benefit others; they were never kind;
 they exploited the poor, the suffering, and the brokenhearted,
 driving them to an early death.

17 They filled their hearts with judgmentalism and curses
     and will reap the curses they sowed;
   their hearts never chose to bless others,
     thus, no blessing ever took root within them.
18 They adorned their characters with curses—
     like water hydrates the body or oil saturates dry bones.
19 Their selfishness is a curse covering their entire being—
     a binding that constantly enslaves them.
20 May the Lord let my adversaries reap the harvest they have sown—
     all those who speak evil about me.
21 But you, O Creator God,
     heal my brokenness with your character of love;
     because you are goodness and love, transform me.
22 For I am afflicted, poor, and crushed down,
     and my heart is deeply wounded.
23 I am fading away like shadow at dusk;
     I am withering quickly like a locust.
24 My knees are weak from fasting;
     my body is skin and bones.
25 My accusers ridicule me;
     when they see me, they shake their heads with scorn.
26 Help me, O Lord my God;
     as the outworking of your faithful love, save me.
27 Then they will know that it is by your power of love
     that you, O Creator God, have done it.
28 They may curse, but you will bless;
     when they attack,
   they will expose their terminal condition and be ashamed,
     but your suffering-servant will rejoice.
29 My accusers cover themselves with disgrace
     and wrap themselves in shame.
30 With my mouth I will pour out thanks to the Lord;
     among the eternal throng I will praise him.
31 For he stands right next to those in need
     to heal them from their terminal sin-sick condition. ◌

PSALM 110
THE LORD STANDS BESIDE YOU TO HELP YOU

[1]   The Lord says to my Lord:
     "Sit beside me, at my right hand,
  until I make your enemies
     a footstool for your feet."
[2]   From Zion, your power of truth and love will extend
     and you will have dominion in the midst of your enemies.
[3]   Your people voluntarily surrender in trust to you;
     on the day when your power of truth and love is fully revealed—
  blazing forth in the beauty of holiness,
     emanating from the source of all life—
     life will start afresh, like dew on a new morning.
[4]   The Lord has made a solemn promise
     and will not change his mind:
  "You are a priest forever—the minister of God's healing Remedy—
     in the order of Melchizedek."
[5]   The Lord stands beside you to help you;
     he will crush the reign of selfishness on the day of his wrath:
[6]   he will diagnose the selfish as terminal, their bodies piled high,
     and crush the head of this world of sin.
[7]   Messiah the King will reign victorious
     and drink from the river of life flowing on the earth made new. ☙

Psalm 111

Quick to Save, He Brings Remedy to His People

1 All praise be to the Lord!

Acclaim and adoration I give to the Lord with all my heart
Before the assembly of the healed—the congregation of the cured.

2 Colossal and wonderful are the methods of the Lord;
Diligently studied by all who delight in them.

3 Excellent and magnificent is all that he creates;
Forever enduring is his righteous character of love.

4 God established a memorial to remember his wonderful creation built on love;
He is kind and merciful.

5 Indwelling the righteous, he feeds the souls of those who revere him;
Jehovah is always focused on fulfilling his promise to heal humankind.

6 Kindly, he has shown his transforming power to the people,
Leading them to inherit the world.

7 Magnificent are his methods of truth and governance;
Never-changing and reliable are his design-laws for life.

8 O, how eternal, perpetual and everlasting they are,
Perfected in truth and righteousness.

9 Quick to save, he brings remedy to his people;
Resolutely, he sustains his healing plan forever—
Supreme and perfect is his character of love.

10 The way of wisdom is to revere, admire and live in harmony with the Lord;
Understanding is found by all who follow God's principles;
Victory and eternal praise belong to him. ❧

Psalm 112

Set right with God, we live in happiness

1 All praise be to the Lord!

   Altogether happy are people who live in harmony with the Lord,
   Because they find eternal healing as they delight in his law.
2 **C**rowned victorious, their children will be mighty in love upon the earth;
   Descendants, set right with God, will live in happiness.
3 **E**ternal prosperity and heavenly treasure is theirs;
   Forever righteous they stay.
4 **G**lorious light shines through the darkness for those set right with God,
   Healing descends from him for the merciful, kind and true.
5 **I**ndeed, good comes to the generous who freely lend—
   Just and honest they are in all their dealings.
6 **K**nowing God, they will not be corrupted with selfishness;
   Loving others, the righteous will always be remembered.
7 **M**astering themselves, they don't live in fear of bad news;
   New hearts are theirs, fixed in trust of God.
8 **O**vercomers, their hearts are sealed to God so they have no fear,
   Preserved in purity in the view of their enemies.
9 **Q**uick to share, they give generously to the poor;
   Renewed by God, their righteousness endures forever,
   Sanctified character keeps them exalted and glorified.
10 **T**he wicked will see and be infuriated;
   Unhealed, they have no excuse and wither away to nothing;
   Vain hope—all their dreams and plans will perish forever. ◌

PSALM 113

HE RAISES FROM DUST THOSE DYING IN SIN

1   Praise the Lord.
    Give praise, all who speak the truth about God;
        shine brightly, revealing the character and methods of the Lord.
2   Let God's character of love be praised
        both now and forevermore.
3   Throughout all creation—from east to west—
        God's character of love is praiseworthy.
4   The Creator is supreme—greater than all nations;
        his glory is higher than the heavens.
5   Who is like our Creator God,
        the Infinite One who sits enthroned high above our reality,
6   who must bend down from infinity
        to look upon the heavens and the earth?
7   He raises from dust those dying in sin
        and exalts those who need healing from decay;
8   he seats them upon thrones,
        with his royal family redeemed from the earth.
9   He makes the barren place home—
        a happy motherland filled with his children.
    Praise the Lord. ℘

Psalm 114

The earth dances at the presence of the Creator

1. When Israel was brought out of Egypt—
   the descendants of Jacob from a foreign power;
2. Judah became God's agency to carry out his healing plan,
   Israel—the avenue for his kingdom of love.
3. The sea recognized God's presence and fled,
   the Jordan also parted;
4. the mountains skipped like rams,
   the hills quaked like young lambs.
5. Why did the sea flee
   or the Jordan part,
6. or the mountains skip like rams
   or the hills quake like young lambs?
7. The earth dances at the presence of the Creator—
   at the presence of the God of Jacob,
8. who turned a rock into a pool of water;
   yes, a solid rock into a spring of water. ❧

PSALM 115

HE IS OUR PROTECTOR AND REMEDY

1   To you alone, O Creator God, to you alone
      and not to us must all glory and honor be given
      because of your character of love and unwavering trustworthiness.

2   How can the nations be so blind and say,
      "Where is their God?"

3   Our God is in heaven
      and he actually lives, and therefore does all that he desires.

4   But their idols are non-living matter—silver and gold
      shaped and fashioned by their own hands.

5   They have carved mouths that cannot speak,
      sculpted eyes that cannot see;

6   they have engraved ears that cannot hear,
      molded noses that cannot smell;

7   they have chiseled hands that cannot feel,
      etched feet that cannot walk;
      nor can they make even the slightest sound with their throats.

8   Those who make them will become like them,
      as will all who worship and trust in them.

9   O people called by God, trust in the Lord—
      he is our protector and remedy.

10   O priesthood of believers, trust in the Lord—
      he is our protector and remedy.

11   All who revere him, trust in the Lord—
      he is our protector and remedy.

12   The Lord knows what we need and he will provide it;
      he provides blessings to the people he has called,
      he provides blessings to the priesthood of believers,

13   he provides blessings to those who revere the Lord—
      young and old alike.

14   The Lord will increase the blessings upon you—
      you and your descendants.

15   May you be blessed by the Lord,
      the Creator of heaven and earth.

¹⁶ The Lord governs the highest heavens,
   but he gave earth to human beings to rule.
¹⁷ The dead do not praise the Lord—
   those who go down to silence;
¹⁸ it is we, the living, who praise the Lord
   both now and forevermore.
   Praise the Lord. ☙

PSALM 116

THE LORD IS GRACIOUS AND SEEKS TO SET HIS CREATION RIGHT

¹ I love the Lord, for he cares about me and listens;
   he hears me every time I call for his help.
² Because he cares about me and listens to me,
   I will talk with him every day of my life.
³ The fear of death overwhelmed me,[12]
   the terror of my terminal condition took hold of me;
   I was trapped in crushing sorrow.
⁴ So, knowing the character of the Lord, I called to him:
   "O Lord, heal me—save me!"
⁵ The Lord is gracious and always seeks to set his creation right;
   our God is love.
⁶ The Lord preserves the individualities of all who have simple trust in him;
   when I acknowledged my great need, he saved me.
⁷ My troubled heart returned to peace,
   because the Lord gave me mature, Godlike character. [13]
⁸ He has cured my terminal condition, saving me from death—
   taking away the sorrow and fear that blinded me—
   and he has stopped me from falling.

---

[12] According to various Hebrew lexicons, the Hebrew word לְבֶה [ḥě·běl] is translated as rope, noose, fate. The various English Bible versions translate this word in this text as: sorrows (KJV), danger (GNT), cords (NIV84), snares (NRSV, ESV), ropes (HCSB). I have used fear, as Scripture tells us that it is the fear of death that is the actual element which keeps us enslaved and Jesus died to "free those who all their lives were held in slavery by their fear of death." (Hebrews 2:15 NIV84).

[13] The Hebrew word גָּמַל [gamal] is translated by various lexicons as "ripen" or "wean," which means to grow up and mature.

9   I live a new life in harmony with the Lord
      in the land of the living.
10   I trusted the Lord when I said,
      "I am dying—my condition is terminal,"
11   even when my fear tempted me to say,
      "No one can be trusted."
12   What can I give to the Lord
      for all the goodness he has given to me?
13   I will carry to others his remedy to save them
      and proclaim God's healing character of love.
14   I will keep my promise to the Lord
      to share his remedy with all the nations.
15   How costly it is to the Lord
      when one of his people dies.
16   O Lord, I am your man!
      I serve you, just as my mother did;
      by you I am healed and set free.
17   I will present a thank offering to you;
      I will proclaim God's character of love.
18   I will keep my promise to the Lord
      to share his remedy with all the nations,
19   in the courts of the Lord's house
      and throughout all Jerusalem.
    Praise the Lord. ❧

PSALM 117

THE TRUSTWORTHINESS OF THE LORD ENDURES FOREVER

1   Accept the Lord and praise him, all you nations;
      accept him and be healed, all you peoples.
2   For his love for us is infinite,
      and the trustworthiness of the Lord endures forever.
    Praise the Lord. ❧

PSALM 118

HIS LOVE IS PERPETUAL AND EVERLASTING

1   Give thanks to the Lord, for he is good;
    his love is perpetual and everlasting.
2   Let those who overcome in union with God, say:
    "His love is perpetual and everlasting."
3   Let the whole priesthood of believers say:
    "His love is perpetual and everlasting."
4   Let those who revere the Lord say:
    "His love is perpetual and everlasting."
5   In my distress I called out to the Lord,
    and he responded by setting me free.
6   The Lord is for me; I will not live in fear.
    What can human beings do to me?
7   The Lord is for me; he is my helper—
    he shows me who my true enemies are.
8   It is better to trust in the Lord
    than to rely on people.
9   It is better to trust in the Lord
    than to rely on world leaders.
10 The selfish world presses in around me,
    but by God's power of love and truth I am cut free of them.
11 They surround me on every side,
    but by God's power of love and truth I am cut free of them.
12 They swarm around me like bees,
    but their lives are quickly expended like burning thorns;
    by God's power of love and truth I am cut free of them.
13 They pushed so hard against me that I was about to fall,
    but the Lord helped me.
14 The Lord is my strength—my source of life—O how I sing for joy;
    he has healed me.
15 Songs of joy and deliverance resound in the homes of those who are healed—
    restored to God's design for life;
    the Lord's Remedy—his Right Hand—has achieved the victory!
16 The Lord's Remedy—his Right Hand—overcomes;

the Lord's Remedy—his Right Hand—produces perfect character!

17 I will not die; I will continue to live
and tell what the Lord has done.
18 The Lord's discipline was painful but therapeutic;
he has healed me, saving me from death.
19 Open for me the gate to perfect restoration to God's design for life,
and I will gladly go in and give all honor and thanks to the Lord.
20 This gate is the Lord,
through whom the healed enter.
21 I give you thanks for answering me;
you are my remedy—my salvation.
22 The stone rejected by the builders
has become the foundation stone of life itself;
23 God has made sure it would be this way,
and it is incredible to us.
24 This is the day of victory, that the Lord has made;
let us rejoice and be glad in it.
25 Now, Lord, save us now!
Now, Lord, heal us completely!
26 Blessed is the One who comes with the character of God!
From the house of the Lord we bless you.
27 The Lord is Creator God,
he shines the light of heavenly truth upon us.
Weave his healing remedy into your life, bind it to your heart—
to cleanse the horns of selfishness infecting the altar of your soul.
28 You are my God, and I will give you thanks;
you are my God, and I will proclaim your character and methods.
29 Give thanks to the Lord, for he is good;
his love is perpetual and everlasting. ଓ

PSALM 119

I DEPEND UPON YOU TO RESTORE YOUR LAW WITHIN ME

א Aleph

1. Happy and healthy are those whose characters have been healed,
    who live in harmony with God's design for life.
2. Happy and healthy are those who preserve God's principles in their characters
    and seek him with all their heart.
3. They do no wrong—
    they walk in the Lord's ways.
4. You have established the laws upon which life and health are built,
    and they are to be eagerly observed.
5. Oh, how I wish my nature was established
    to naturally live in harmony with your design protocols for life!
6. Then I would not feel ashamed
    when I compare my life to your perfect law of love.
7. When your living law of love is assimilated into my mind and character,
    I will praise you with a heart that is right with you.
8. I will live in harmony with your specifications for life;
    please don't let go of me.

ב Beth

9. How can a young person keep their life pure?
    By living in harmony with your word—your design for life.
10. I am on a journey to find you, seeking you with all my heart;
    don't let me stray from your directions.
11. I have internalized your methods into my life,
    that I may never betray you.
12. I kneel in adoration before you, O Lord;
    teach me all your ways.
13. I recite aloud
    all the therapeutic directives you have given us.
14. In living out your methods I find the greatest joy,
    beyond all riches.
15. I meditate on your design protocols for life
    and study the way you function.
16. I delight in all your prescriptions;
    I will not forget what you have taught me.

ג Gimel

17 Develop and mature your servant, that I might thrive
and live in harmony with your design-law for life.
18 Open my mind, that I may truly see
the wonderful ways in which your law is built into all reality.
19 I am like a foreigner in the land—one who doesn't know the customs—
so please don't hide your instructions from me.
20 My heart is starving, constantly longing
to have your standard for life and health fully restored within me.
21 You rebuke the self-centered—the miserable and spiritually sick
who cling to error and violate your design.
22 Free me from the ridicule and condemnation I experience
because I carefully apply all you say.
23 Though leaders get together and gossip about me,
I, your representative, will study your methods.
24 Your design-laws are my delight—
my hedge of protection and a guidepost.

ד Daleth

25 My heart is infected with selfishness; it is terminal and dying.
Heal me—infuse me with life, restoring your design-law of love within me.
26 I have confessed my brokenness—how I naturally do things the selfish way—
and you came to me to train me in your methods of love.
27 Enable me to understand how you built reality to operate,
then I will meditate on your wonderful ways.
28 I am dying under the weight of sin;
revive me with your truth.
29 Remove from me all falsehood and misunderstanding,
and graciously give me your law of love.
30 I have chosen the way of truth;
I am committed to your design for life.
31 I hold fast to your methods, O Lord,
and I am not ashamed.
32 I eagerly live in harmony with your design,
for you have healed my heart, enabling me to do so.

ה He

33 Teach me, O Lord, the way you have designed life to operate,
    so that I might conform and be transformed.
34 Enable me to understand, and I will practice your principles
    and live out your methods with all my heart.
35 Lead me to live according to your ways,
    because it brings me health and happiness.
36 Transform my heart to desire your methods of love
    and hate selfish gain.
37 Turn my interest away from all worthless things;
    recreate me to live according to your way.
38 Establish your promise within your servant,
    so that you may be worshipped and admired.
39 Heal me, take away my disgrace and fear,
    for your ways are always good.
40 O how I have longed for your methods!
    Give me eternal life through your perfect righteousness.

I Waw

41 Renew me with your perfect character of love, O Lord,
    the transformation and healing you promised—
42 a perfected life that rebuts the accuser—
    for I trust your word.
43 Never stop feeding me your healing truth,
    for I depend upon you to restore your law within me.
44 Then I will live in harmony with your design for life
    for all eternity future.
45 I will live in true freedom,
    for I have internalized your methods.
46 I will declare your design-laws before world leaders,
    and I will not be ashamed.
47 My greatest delight is living out your methods,
    because I love them.
48 I reach out with all my power to embrace your ways, which I love,
    and I meditate on your designs.

ז Zayin

49 Remember your promise to me, your servant,
for you are my only hope.
50 My hope in you comforts me in the midst of trouble,
for your words are living threads of life-giving energy.
51 The conceited always make fun of me,
but I will not deviate from your design for life.
52 I remember your law—the perpetual principles that govern life;
O how they bring me comfort, my Lord.
53 Seeing the self-injury and character corruption of the wicked,
who violate your design-laws, fills me with horror and indignation.
54 My life is a song and your instructions are the melody
that directs the music of my life.
55 Each night I reflect on your character of love, O Lord,
and I treasure your methods and principles.
56 This joy is mine,
for I preserve your living law in my heart.

ח Heth

57 You, O Lord, are my life;
I choose you—I choose to follow all your instructions.
58 With all my heart I seek your presence;
pour your healing grace upon me and prepare me, just as you have promised.
59 I have considered my selfish condition—my ways—
and have chosen to follow your methods of love.
60 Eagerly, without delay, I hasten
to live in harmony with your laws—the way you built life to operate.
61 Bands of selfish people seek to captivate me from every side,
but I will not turn away from your law of love.
62 When I awake in the night, I give thanks to you,
because you govern righteously.
63 I am a friend to all who revere you,
to all who live in harmony with your methods and principles.
64 The earth is built upon your living law of love, O Creator God;
teach me your perfect ways.

ט Teth

65 You have done what is best for me, your servant, O Lord,
> just as you have promised.

66 Give me wisdom to understand reality—how you have built life to operate—
> for I trust the way you have ordered life.

67 Before I felt the painful consequences, I used to wander from your ways,
> but now I live in harmony with your designs.

68 You are good and do only good;
> teach me to live like you.

69 The self-centered smear me with lies
> because I live out your law of love with all my heart.

70 Their hearts are calloused, bloated with selfishness,
> but I thrive in harmonizing with your design-law.

71 It was therapeutic for me to suffer painful consequences,
> so that I might learn how your creation works.

72 Your instructions are more precious to me
> than billions in gold and silver.

י Yodh

73 You have held me in your hands and made me who I am;
> give me the ability to learn your ways.

74 May those who revere your methods of love rejoice when they see me,
> for I have waited for your healing remedy.

75 I know, O Creator God, that your design-laws are right—the standard for life—
> and your faithfulness in sustaining them lets me reap the suffering I chose.

76 May your healing love comfort me,
> just as you promised me, your servant.

77 May your merciful remedy come to me, that I may live,
> for your design for life is my true delight.

78 May the self-centered be ashamed for lying about me,
> but I will meditate upon your principles.

79 May those who embrace your methods of love be reunited with me—
> all those who understand your design for life.

80 May my character be perfectly restored to harmony with your law of love,
> that I may not be ashamed.

ך Kaph

81 I desperately hunger for your healing;
    I await your perfect remedy.
82 I am tired of waiting to be well, of waiting for your promise to be fulfilled;
    I wonder, "When will you fully heal my heart?"
83 Though I am old and withered like a leather bag dried in the smoke,
    I do not forget your ways.
84 How long must I go on?
    When will you diagnose those who persecute me as incurable?
85 The self-centered dig traps to cause my downfall—
    those who hate your methods and violate your designs.
86 All your design-laws are reliable constants;
    help me reveal the truth, for people attack my reputation with lies.
87 They nearly ended my earthly life,
    but I refused to compromise and would not deviate from your design.
88 Give me life by your love,
    and I will live as you have testified life should operate.

ל Lamedh

89 Your design-laws, O Creator God, are eternal;
    they are built right into the fabric of the cosmos.
90 Your truth is faithfully revealed to all generations;
    you built the earth, and the evidence stands firm.
91 All nature continues to this day because of your sustaining laws,
    for all evidence and truth serve you.
92 If I did not love and embrace your design-laws,
    I would have died in my own self-induced misery.
93 I will never forget your principles,
    for by restoring them in me you have given me eternal life.
94 Heal me, for I am yours;
    I choose your methods and principles.
95 The selfish hope they can destroy me,
    but I know reality—your design protocols for life.
96 Everything human is finite—limited;
    but your governance is infinite—boundless.

ם Mem

97 Oh, how I love your design—your living law built right into reality!
    I meditate upon it all day long.
98 Your laws make me wiser than my enemies;
    they continually enlighten me.
99 I have greater understanding of reality than all my teachers,
    for I humbly contemplate your law of love.
100 I have greater understanding of reality than the elders,
    for I live in harmony with your principles.
101 I have refused to walk in selfishness—I keep clear of every evil path—
    in order to live in harmony with your instructions.
102 I do not turn away from your cause—your kingdom of love—
    for you have taught me the truth.
103 Oh, how sweet your truth tastes,
    sweeter even than honey!
104 From your design-laws I gain insight into how reality works,
    therefore I hate every path that deviates from your design for life.

ן Nun

105 Your word is the lamp that guides my steps—
    the light that directs my way.
106 I will keep my promise
    to diligently follow the treatment plan you determine is right.
107 I have suffered so much, O Lord;
    heal me—restore me to life, just as you have promised.
108 May the spontaneous speech of my mouth be pleasing to you, O Lord;
    teach me to live your law of love.
109 My life is under constant threat,
    but I will not forget your design for life.
110 The selfish have set traps for me,
    but I do not deviate from your principles of love.
111 Your living law of love is my possession forever;
    it is the joy of my heart.
112 With all my heart I choose to keep your methods of love forevermore,
    for doing so changes everything.

ס Samekh

113 I hate inconsistency, unreliability, disloyalty,
    but I love your design-laws.

114 You are my safe haven, my protective remedy;
    my hope is in your promise.

115 Remove from me all selfishness and those who promote it,
    that I may live in harmony with the design of my Creator God!

116 Infuse me with your life-giving presence just as you promised, and I will live;
    please don't let me spoil what I have hoped for.

117 Heal me and I will be delivered from my terminal condition,
    then I will continually live in harmony with the way you built life to operate.

118 You reject as viable all who persist in deviating from your design for life,
    for all their false remedies are useless.

119 The persistently selfish you excise from the earth like necrotic tissue;
    Oh, how I love your healing methods.

120 I tremble in awe of you;
    I stand in humble admiration of your laws—your design protocols for life.

ע Ayin

121 I have done what is right and good;
    don't leave me to my enemies.

122 Ensure your servant's well-being;
    do not let the selfish oppress me.

123 My eyes strain to see your deliverance,
    to see your promise fulfilled.

124 Transform me by your love
    and teach me your ways.

125 I am yours; give me wisdom
    that I may assimilate and live out your methods.

126 It is time for you to intervene, O Lord,
    for your design for life is being broken.

127 This is the reason I love your methods
    more than all the gold in the world;

128 this is the reason I consider all your precepts right
    and hate everything that breaks your design for life.

פ Pe

129 Your design-laws are wonderful,
>therefore I live in harmony with them.
130 The entrance of your word enlightens the mind
>and teaches the unlearned how reality works.
131 I pant with an open mouth—
>that's how deeply I long for your law of love.
132 Turn to me and pour your healing grace upon me,
>as you always do for those who love you.
133 Guide my choices to be in harmony with your methods;
>do not let selfishness control me.
134 Deliver me from selfishness which oppresses humanity,
>that I may live like you designed.
135 Bless me with greater revelations of yourself
>and teach me your ways.
136 My tears flow like a river,
>because so many people violate your law of life.

צ Tsadhe

137 You are perfect and right, O Lord,
>and the laws you constructed life upon are also perfect and right.
138 The principles you have built into reality are perfect and right;
>they are constants—trustworthy and reliable.
139 I am so upset I am worn out,
>because my enemies refuse your instructions.
140 Your word is absolutely true and reliable,
>and oh, how I love it.
141 I am weak and unimportant,
>but I do not forget your principles.
142 Your righteousness is everlasting righteousness,
>and your design-law is the truth—the way reality operates.
143 Trouble and distress inevitably find me,
>but I find delight in following your prescription for living.
144 Your methods are always right;
>help me understand and embrace them, so I will live.

ק Qoph

145 With all my heart I call out to you, O Lord,
>come to me and I will be enabled to live as you direct.

146 I call to you; heal me,
>and I will carry out your principles.

147 I rise before dawn and cry out for help,
>and I wait on your instructions.

148 I stay awake at night
>and meditate upon your promises.

149 Hear me Lord, because you love me;
>give me life by restoring your design-law within me.

150 Those who live for self, pursuing their me-first agenda,
>are far outside your law of love.

151 Yet you are always near, O Lord,
>and your design-laws are truth—the way reality works.

152 I learned long ago that you established your laws as the foundation of reality,
>and they will last forever.

ר Resh

153 See how sin-sickness torments me, and heal me,
>for I have not rejected love—your law for life.

154 Fight for me and rescue me;
>give me eternal life, just as you have promised.

155 The persistently selfish are far from being cured,
>for they do not seek for your treatment.

156 Your kindness and tenderness are infinite, O Lord;
>give me life by restoring your law within me.

157 I have many enemies who oppose me,
>but I do not stray from your ways.

158 Seeing persistently-selfish sickens me,
>for they rebel against your design for life.

159 See how I love your methods;
>give me life, O Lord, by restoring your love within me.

160 The source of your law is truth;
>your righteous government is eternal.

ש Sin and Shin

[161] Leaders attack me for no reason,
    but I stand in awe of the truth about you, O God.
[162] In my entire being I celebrate your directions—
    it's like finding a map to the greatest treasure.
[163] I hate and detest all false dealings
    but I love your law.
[164] Seven times a day I praise you,
    because your design-laws are perfect.

[165] Great peace have they who love and live your law,
    and they do not stumble.
[166] I wait eagerly for your healing, O Lord,
    while I diligently follow your treatment plan.
[167] I live in harmony with your principles for life,
    And I love them very much.
[168] I practice your methods and follow your instructions,
    for everything I do and think is open before you.

ת Taw

[169] May you grant my heart's desire, O Lord—
    reveal your truth to me and give me understanding of your kingdom.
[170] Grant my plea for mercy
    and heal me just as your promised.
[171] Let praise flow freely from my lips,
    for you taught me your ways.
[172] Let my tongue sing of your revelations of truth,
    for all your laws are perfect—the protocols for life and health.
[173] Your hand always helps me,
    for I have chosen your kingdom of love.
[174] I long for complete healing, O Lord;
    your law is my life, health and happiness.
[175] Give me life that I may glorify you;
    may your laws sustain me.
[176] When I, like a lost sheep, stray from your path,
    please come and find me, and bring me home,
    for I have not rejected your law of love. ✃

PSALM 120
WHEN DISTRESSED, I CALL OUT TO THE LORD

1   When distressed, I call out to the Lord
  and he answers me.
2   Deliver me, O Lord, from all falsehood
  and from all betrayal and backstabbing.
3   What will the Lord do to you,
  who practice deceit and prefer lies?
4   Your consciences will be pierced by the arrows of your own lies
  and your characters charred like burning coals of a dry tree.
5   I am miserable living among the deceitful—
  among those who hate the truth.
6   For far too long I have lived
  among those who hate peace.
7   I long for peace;
  but when I speak, they are for war. ଔ

PSALM 121
HE GUARDS ALL THOSE, WHO WITH GOD, OVERCOME

1   I see the high places of pagan worship all around me,
  but where does my help come from?
2   My help comes from the Lord—
  the Creator of heaven and earth.
3   He will not allow your steps for him to be overthrown—
  he who guards you will never tire or fall asleep.
4   Indeed, he who guards all those, who with God, overcome,
  will never get tired nor sleep.
5   The Lord preserves you—
  the Lord stands beside you, protecting your soul from corruption,
6   protecting you from harm during the sunlight of day
  or the moonlight of night.
7   The Lord will keep your character pure from all evil;
  he will keep guard over your life.
8   The Lord will watch over all you do, both now and forevermore. ଔ

Psalm 122

May complete healing and restoration occur within you

1 I was glad when they said to me,
"Let us go to the Lord's temple."
2 And now we are here,
standing at your gates, O Jerusalem.
3 Jerusalem is a city designed
as a place of unity and loving fellowship.
4 This is where the people gather—
the people who love God—
to praise and celebrate the character of God
acting out his plan of healing, as given to Israel.
5 There, the descendants of David
set their thrones to govern the people.
6 Pray for the success of Jerusalem,
that those who love this city be healthy and happy;
7 that there will be restoration to godliness within its walls—
that trust and friendship will be its fortress.
8 For all my family and friends, I say,
"May complete healing and restoration occur within you."
9 In harmony with the purpose of God's temple,
I will seek your eternal welfare.

Psalm 123

The Creator God governs all reality from heaven

1 I look to you, the Creator God, who governs all reality from heaven.
2 As a servant depends upon his master,
as a maid depends upon her mistress,
so we look to our Creator God,
depending upon his love and mercy.
3 Have mercy and heal us, O Lord; have mercy and deliver us,
for we have endured so much mistreatment.
4 We have tired, worn out from being ridiculed by the selfish
and mocked by the arrogant.

PSALM 124

OUR DELIVERANCE COMES FROM THE GOD OF LOVE

1 What would have happened if the Lord had not been for us?
   Let all Israel say this:
2 What would have happened if the Lord had not been for us
   when people rose against us?
3 They would have devoured us
   when their anger burned against us;
4 the flood would have drowned us,
   the torrents washed over us,
5 the raging waters
   would have swept us away.
6 Give thanks to the Lord,
   who did not let our enemies destroy us.
7 We have escaped like a bird
   out of a hunter's cage:
   the cage has been broken,
   and we are set free.
8 Our deliverance comes from the God of love—
   the Creator of heaven and earth. ∞

PSALM 125

THOSE WHO TRUST IN THE LORD ARE A STRONGHOLD OF LOVE

1 Those who trust in the Lord are a stronghold of love—like Mount Zion;
   they cannot be shaken but will endure forever.
2 As the mountains surround and protect Jerusalem,
   so the Lord surrounds and protects his people both now and forevermore.
3 The power of selfishness will not rule over the righteous,
   for the godly will not choose to do wrong.
4 Do good, O Lord, to those who love good—
   to those whose hearts are in tune with you.
5 But all who cling to selfishness
   the Lord will let go, along with all who prefer evil.
   Health and salvation to all, who with God, overcome. ∞

Psalm 126

The Creator God Has Done an Incredible Work

¹ When the Lord turned around the backsliding of Zion,
 we were like people whose dreams of health came true.
² Then our mouths were filled with laughter
 and we shouted for joy;
then it was said among the unhealed,
 "The Creator God has done an incredible work of transformation for them."
³ The Creator has done an incredible work of transformation in us;
 Oh, how happy we are!
⁴ Restore our health and well-being, O Lord,
 just as streams bring life to the desert.
⁵ Those who break the stony heart to sow the seeds of truth
 will reap a joyful harvest.
⁶ Those who go through life with tender hearts,
 carrying seeds of truth to sow,
will come home filled with joy,
 bringing in an abundant harvest. ❧

Psalm 127

Unless the Lord builds the house, it will not stand

1 Unless the Lord builds the house,
  it will not stand.
Unless the Lord governs a city,
  it will collapse into ruin.
2 It is useless to wake up worried,
  to fret late into the night,
to be anxious at every meal—
  for God provides for his loved ones even while they sleep.
3 The heritage designed by God are children—
  the reward of giving birth.
4 Like arrows in the hands of a warrior
  are children in a growing family.
5 Happy are the parents
  whose quiver is full of them,
for they will not be defeated
  when they contend with their enemies at the gate. ☙

Psalm 128

Happy and healthy are those who revere the Lord

1 Happy and healthy are those who revere the Lord
  and live according to his design for life.
2 Your work will strengthen and develop you;
  it will be good for you, and you will be happy.
3 Your wife will bless and nurture your home;
  your children will bring wonder and promise to your table.
4 Yes, those who revere the Lord
  will be blessed by living in harmony with his designs.
5 May the Lord send you blessings from his dwelling place,
  that you may see God's people prosper every day of your life,
6 and live to see you grandchildren.
  Peace upon all, who with God, overcome. ☙

Psalm 129

The blessing of the Lord is upon you

1. Since our very beginning as a people, we have been oppressed—
   let Israel say—
2. since our very beginning as a people, we have been oppressed,
   but they have not defeated us.
3. They have cut deep wounds in our backs—
   like a field plowed deep with furrows—
4. but our righteous Lord
   has freed us from slavery.
5. All who hate Zion
   will be ashamed and turned away.
6. They will be like grass on a roof—cut off from the source of life—
   which withers and dies;
7. it produces no grain
   and is unfit for harvest.
8. Those who pass by will be unable to say,
   "The blessing of the Lord is upon you;
   we pronounce the Lord's blessing upon you." ⚘

Psalm 130

He himself will heal and save his people

1 From the depths of despair I cry out to you, O Lord!
2 Hear my plea, O Lord;
   pay close attention
   to my deep need of your healing mercy.
3 O Creator God, if you kept a record of sins,
   who could avoid legal condemnation?
4 But you forgive freely and heal what is wrong,
   therefore you are loved and revered.
5 I rely on the Lord with my entire being,
   and I trust in his remedy.
6 I long for the Lord
   more than watchmen wait for the morning—
   yes, more than watchmen wait for the morning.
7 O people of God, put your trust in the Lord,
   for the Lord is the source of infinite, never-failing love,
   and from him is full restoration to perfect, everlasting life.
8 He himself will heal and save his people
   from all their sinfulness. ଓ

Psalm 131

O people of God, trust the Lord

1 O Lord, I am no better than anyone else;
   I see all human beings as equal before your eyes.
   I do not exercise my strength outside your will for my life
   or pursue positions beyond what you have equipped me to fulfill.
2 Instead, I am content and at peace—
   like a weaned child no longer crying for mother's milk;
   like a weaned child, I am content and at peace.
3 O people of God, trust the Lord
   both now and forevermore. ଓ

Psalm 132

He will provide all that is needed

1 O Lord, remember David—
    his heart was afflicted because of his love for you.[14]
2 Remember, Lord, his promise—
    the vow he made to the Mighty God of Jacob:
3 "I will not retire to my home
    or lay around in my bed,
4 or experience a peaceful sleep
    or a satisfied rest
5 until I find a place to build a house for the Lord—
    a sanctuary for the Mighty God of Jacob."
6 We heard about the ark while in Ephrathah,
    but we found it in the fields of Jaar.
7 We will enter the Lord's sacred healing place
    and worship at his footstool.
8 Establish, O Lord, your resting place—
    the place for your ark, the symbol of your healing power.
9 May all who minister your remedy be clothed in your character of love;
    may your healed people sing for joy.
10 For the sake of David, your loyal follower,
    do not reject your Anointed One.
11 The Lord made a solemn vow to David,
    a promise that he will not break:
    "One of your own descendants
    will reign on your throne.
12 If your descendants take my remedy and follow my treatment plan,
        living in harmony with my design protocols for life I teach them,
    then their descendants
        will reign on your throne for ever and ever."
13 For the Lord has chosen Zion,
        he has desired it as the distribution hub for his remedy to sin:
14 "This is where I want to live forever;

---

[14] Much of David's suffering was due to his honoring the Lord's plan and timing, and refusal to rebel against Saul, the Lord's anointed.

this is where I want my government of love to be established.
15 I will provide all that is needed for my plan to succeed;
   I will feed all who hunger.
16 I will clothe with eternal life those who minister my remedy,
   and all who accept my healing will sing for joy.
17 Here I will make David's descendant both Remedy and King,
   and my Anointed One will enlighten my people.
18 I will cover his enemies with shame,
   but he himself will be crowned with life everlasting." ❧

PSALM 133
GOD IMPARTS HIS REMEDY INTO THE HEARTS OF PEOPLE

1 How beautiful and pleasant it is
   when God's people live together in harmony!
2 This happens when the oil of love and truth cleanse the mind
   (oil poured on the head),
saturate the growth and development
   (running down on the beard),
saturate the growth and development of our leaders
   (running down on Aaron's beard),
and become part of the character
   (running down upon his robes).
3 It is like the life-giving love from heaven
   (like the dew of Hermon)
falling upon the people
   (falling on Mount Zion).
Into the hearts of people is where God imparts his remedy,
   healing them to everlasting life. ❧

PSALM 134

SURRENDER YOURSELVES TO HOLINESS

1 Praise the Lord, all you who serve the Lord,
    all who stand watch in the Lord's house through the darkness.
2 Surrender yourselves to holiness
    and praise the Lord.
3 May the Lord, the Creator of heaven and earth,
    bless you from Zion. ⊂⊃

PSALM 135

PRAISE BE TO THE LORD FROM ZION

1 Praise the Lord!
Praise the Lord's character of love;
    praise him, all you who serve the Lord,
2 you who stand watch in the Lord's house of healing,
    in the courts of the Lord's treatment center—his temple.
3 Praise the Lord, for he is good;
    sing praises to his perfect character of love, for it is delightful.
4 For the Lord has chosen Jacob to be his treatment team,
    Israel as the avenue for his treasured remedy.
5 I know that the Lord is great—he created all reality,
    and thus the Lord is greater than all gods.
6 The Lord delighted in creating the entire universe,
    the heavens and the earth,
    the seas and all the deep oceans—all upon the principle of love.
7 He designed the waters to rise and form clouds all across the earth
    to bring rain along with lightning;
    from his treasury of living plants, he brings the air we breathe.
8 Yet he put the firstborn of Egypt in the grave—
    the firstborn of both people and animals.
9 He sent abundant evidence and amazing miracles
    revealing the truth to you, O Egypt—

to Pharaoh and all who worshipped him.
10 He defeated many pagan nations
    and destroyed the might of those worldly kings—
11 Sihon king of the Amorites,
    Og king of Bashan,
    and all the kings of Canaan—
12 and gave their land to others to possess;
    to possess by Israel, his spiritual health-care team.
13 O Lord, your character of love endures forever;
    your reputation, O Lord, through all generations.
14 The Lord will accurately diagnose his people
    and take comfort in healing those who trust and serve him.
15 The idols of other nations are nothing but non-living matter—
    just silver and gold,
    molded and shaped by their own human hands.
16 They have carved mouths that cannot speak,
    sculpted eyes that cannot see;
17 they have engraved ears that cannot hear,
    and they do not breathe.
18 Those who make them will become like them,
    as will all who worship and trust in them.
19 O people called by God, praise the Lord;
    O worship-leaders, praise the Lord;
20 O priesthood of believers, praise the Lord;
    all who revere him, praise the Lord.
21 Praise be to the Lord from Zion—
    to him who established the foundation of peace.
    Praise the Lord. ❧

PSALM 136

HIS LOVE GIVES LIFE FOREVER

1 Give thanks to the Lord, for he is good.
    His love gives life forever.
2 Give thanks to the only true God.
    His love gives life forever.
3 Give thanks to the Lord of lords:
    His love gives life forever.
4 to him who alone built the universe from nothing;
    His love gives life forever.
5 to him who alone had the wisdom to make the heavens;
    His love gives life forever.
6 to him who brought forth land from the deep waters;
    His love gives life forever.
7 to him who created the great lights—
    His love gives life forever.
8 the sun to rule the day,
    His love gives life forever.
9 the moon and stars to rule the night;
    His love gives life forever.
10 to him who defeated the power of Egypt through their firstborn
    His love gives life forever.
11 and brought Israel out from among them
    His love gives life forever.
12 with a mighty display of power and protective hand;
    His love gives life forever.
13 to him who parted the Red Sea
    His love gives life forever.
14 and led Israel safely through it
    His love gives life forever.
15 but swept Pharaoh and his army into the Red Sea;
    His love gives life forever.
16 to him who led his people through the wilderness,
    His love gives life forever.

17 who defeated great kings
      His love gives life forever.
18 and destroyed the pomp and might of those worldly kings—
      His love gives life forever.
19 Sihon king of the Amorites
      His love gives life forever.
20 and Og king of Bashan—
      His love gives life forever.
21 and gave their land to others to possess
      His love gives life forever.
22 (to Israel, his spiritual health-care team);
      His love gives life forever.
23 to the One who remembered us when we were helpless
      His love gives life forever.
24 and freed us from our enemies,
      His love gives life forever.
25 who provides food for all living things.
      His love gives life forever.
26 Give thanks to the Creator God of heaven.
      His love gives life forever. ❧

PSALM 137

SONGS FROM CAPTIVITY

1 By the rivers of Babylon, as captives in this selfish world, we wept
    when we remembered Zion—
    God's fortress of spiritual health and wellness.
2 There on the willows
    we hung our harps
3 while our captors told us to sing:
    they demanded songs of happiness and joy;
    they said, "Sing us a song of health about Zion!"
4 How can our lives be songs revealing God's character of love
    while our hearts are held captive to this selfish world?
5 If I forget the truth about you, O Jerusalem—
    the center of God's healing plan—
    may I write no more music.
6 May I sing no more songs,
    if they are not about you—
    if they do not teach God's healing plan centered in you, O Jerusalem,
    as my highest joy.
7 Remember, O Lord, what the Edomites did
    the day Jerusalem—your spiritual treatment center—fell?
    They shouted, "Tear it down,
    tear it down to the ground!"
8 O people of Babylon, who cling to selfishness,
    you are doomed to destruction!
    Happy are those who are finished with you, just as you deserve;
    who have weaned themselves from you.
9 Happy are they who take your children
    to fall upon the Rock and be broken. ◌

PSALM 138

HIS METHODS OF TRUTH AND LOVE NEVER CHANGE

1 With all my heart I give you thanks, O Creator God,
  before the heavenly assembly I sing your praise.
2 I humble myself to your healing presence as taught by your holy temple,
  and I praise your character of love;
for your methods of truth and love never change,
  and your promise confirms that your character of love
  is supreme over all creation.
3 The day I acknowledged my need and called for help, you answered me;
  you gave me confidence and strength to do what is right.
4 May all the rulers of the earth give thanks to you, O Lord,
  when they hear the truth you have spoken.
5 May their lives be songs revealing the methods of the Lord,
  for the Lord's glorious character of love is supreme.
6 Though the Lord is exalted on high, he cares for the humble,
  but he knows that the proud keep their distance.
7 Though I live in the midst of a world of troubles,
  you heal me to live eternally;
you send your Hand to stand against my enemies—
  through the One at your right hand you save me.
8 The Lord will complete his healing work in me;
  your love, O Lord, gives life forever—
  don't give up on restoring your creation. ❧

PSALM 139

LORD, YOU SUSTAIN ALL REALITY

¹ O Lord, you have examined me
  and you know everything about me.
² You know every action I take;
  from across the cosmos, you know every thought I think.
³ You know whether I am working or resting;
  you know my heart motives—the way I operate.
⁴ Before the words come out of my mouth
  you know exactly what I will say, O Lord.
⁵ You seek me to lead me—you surround me,
  guiding me and protecting me.
⁶ The full knowledge of you is too immense for me;
  you are infinite, and I cannot comprehend it.
⁷ Where can I go and be away from your Spirit?
  You sustain all reality—where can I flee and be beyond your presence?
⁸ If I go to heaven, your sustaining presence is there;
  if I sleep in the grave, your sustaining presence is there as well.
⁹ If I rise with the beams of sunlight in the east,
  if I settle beyond the ocean waves in the west—
¹⁰ even there your hand would guide me,
  the One at your right hand would keep me safe.
¹¹ I could claim that darkness will hide me
  and the light around me turn to night,
¹² but my claim doesn't change reality and no darkness is impenetrable to you;
  for night becomes day in your presence, and darkness becomes light.
¹³ For you have redeemed my heart and mind; ¹⁵

---

¹⁵ The Hebrew word translated in many Bible versions as "formed" or "made" is קָנָה [qanah], and according to the New American Standard Hebrew-Aramaic and Greek Dictionaries, is translated most commonly as "bought," "buy," "purchased," and also as "redeemed." The Hebrew word translated as "inmost being" is כְּלָיָה [kilyah/kil·yaw/] and means "seat of emotions or affections," thus the author's translation of "heart and mind." The Hebrew word translated as "knit me together" according to the Enhanced Strong's Lexicon is סוּךְ, סוּךְ, סָכַךְ, סָכַךְ, סָכַךְ, שָׂכַךְ [cakak, sakak /saw·kak/] v. A primitive root; TWOT 1475, 1492, 2259, 2260; GK 6056 and 6058 and 6114 and 6115 and 6116 and 8503; 23 occurrences; AV translates it as "cover" 15 times, "covering" twice, "defence" once, "defendest" once, "hedge in" once, "join together" once, "set" once, and "shut up" once." Contrary to popular translations, the context of this verse is not about physical embryological development, or God using power to physically create a new human life, but is about the plan of redemption. The Psalmist in Psalms 51:5 describes that he was "born in sin, conceived in iniquity" and here acknowledges that despite his sinful origins, God was already there acting to redeem him and cleanse him from sinfulness.

you covered me with grace
from the moment I was conceived in my mother's womb.
14   I praise you because you are awesome;
wonderful and marvelous are all your works,
and I know this very well.
15   You know my entire being—
how I was built from your secret code,
constructed from the elements of the earth.
16   You saw me before I was born;
my entire life was recorded in your book of foreknowledge
before one day came to be.
17   To me, your thoughts and purposes are the most precious, O God—
the infinite source of all reality;
18   if I could count them,
they would outnumber all the grains of sand.
No matter what I think or do,
it bears witness to your foreknowledge.
19   When will you destroy selfishness, O God?
Remove from me all those who love death—
the violation of your law of life;
20   for the selfish scheme
to promote lies—false remedies—in your kingdom.
21   I abhor how they hate you, O Lord;
I am sick of seeing them work against you!
22   I despise their lies and selfishness—I absolutely hate it!
I recognize they are enemies to love and truth.
23   Examine me, O God, and know the deepest recesses of my heart;
test me and identify every troublesome thought.
24   Determine if there is any unhealthy way in me,
and lead me back to everlasting life. ∞

PSALM 140

HE HEALS AND SHIELDS MY MIND FOR DAILY BATTLES

1 Save me, O Lord, from wicked people;
   protect me from those who exploit others:
2 they plot evil in their hearts
   and constantly instigate division and conflict.
3 Like snakes, their tongues slither falsehood, severing the bonds of love—
   the poisonous lies of the serpent Satan are on their lips.
4 Protect me, O Lord, from the power of the selfish;
   keep me safe from those who exploit others,
   who plot my destruction.
5 The arrogant have laid traps for me,
   they have hidden their nets and have spread their snares along my path.
6 I say to the Lord: "You are my God!"
   O Lord, help me when I call.
7 O Creator God—my powerful Remedy—
   who heals and shields my mind for daily battles.
8 do not allow the wicked to have their way,
   do not let their plans succeed.
9 The minds of those who swarm around me
   will be destroyed by their own evil choices.
10 The fires of infinite truth and love will fall upon them;
    they will be thrown into the consuming fire of God's presence,
    disintegrating into oblivion, never to rise again.
11 A liar and slanderer will not endure on the earth;
    evil will destroy the abusers of others.
12 I know the Lord will set right the humble,
    correctly diagnosing those in need.
13 Certainly those restored to your right design will praise your character of love,
    and the healed will live in your presence. ◌

PSALM 141

I LOOK TO YOU AND KEEP MY TRUST IN YOU, O CREATOR GOD

1   O Lord, I call for your help—come quickly to me.
    Respond kindly to my voice when I call to you.
2   Make my prayers pure and sweet, like the most fragrant incense before you;
    I raise my hands, surrendering to your cleansing—
    just like the evening sacrifice depicts.
3   Lord, empower me with the ability to control what I say;
    let me speak nothing that misrepresents you.
4   Turn the desires of my heart away from fear and selfishness,
    away from evil activity;
  don't let me share the pleasures
    of those who do wrong.
5   Let a godly person discipline me—it is a kindness;
    let the healthy person correct me—it is healing salve to my character.
  Don't allow the oil of selfishness to permeate my character;
    my constant prayer is to break the power of wickedness.
6   When at the judgment they realize
    that choosing evil severs their connection to life—
  like falling off a cliff and expecting to live—
    they will learn that what I taught was true.
7   They will admit, "As a plow cuts through the earth,
    so too our evil choices cut us off from life
    and we are consumed by the grave."
8   But I look to you and keep my trust in you, O Creator God;
    in you I seek healing—don't let me die.
9   Keep me from the snares the selfish have laid for me—
    from the traps of the wicked.
10 Those who persist in selfishness will be trapped by their own evil choices,
    while I pass by safely. ⊗

PSALM 142

SET ME FREE FROM MY PRISON OF FEAR AND DISCOURAGEMENT

1. I call out to the Lord for help;
   I cry out to the Lord for his gracious intervention.
2. I tell him what I need;
   I pour before him my troubles.
3. When I am exhausted and ready to give up,
   you know exactly what I need to do.
   Throughout my journey in life
   people have laid traps for me.
4. When I look around me,
   there is no friend to help me
   and no one to protect me—
   no one cares about me.
5. I call to you, O Lord;
   I say, "You are my friend—
   you are all I truly need in this life."
6. Respond to my cry,
   for I am so very discouraged;
   rescue me from my persecutors,
   for they are too strong for me.
7. Set me free from my prison of fear and discouragement,
   that I may celebrate your character of love:
   then the spiritually healthy will be my friends,
   because you have healed my heart. ❧

PSALM 143
TEACH ME TO FULFILL YOUR PURPOSES

1   O Lord, respond favorably to my prayer,
> intervene mercifully to my plea!
> Because you are faithful and always do what is right,
> come to my relief.

2   Do not judge me responsible for my sin-condition,
> for no one living can set themselves right with you.

3   The enemy hounds me,
> crushing my joy for life into the dirt,
> driving me into darkness with no zest for living—
> like those already long dead.

4   I am tired of living,
> I am discouraged and ready to give up,

5   but then I remember what happened in the past—
> I focus upon your design and all you have done
> and think about your plan and all you have made.

6   I surrender myself to you;
> my inmost being thirsts for your life-giving presence
> like dry land thirsts for rain.

7   Respond to me quickly, O Lord;
> I am dying inside.
> Do not keep your life-giving presence from me
> or I will surely die and join those in the grave.

8   Let each day start with your love filling my heart,
> for I have put my trust in you.
> Teach me the way to live,
> for I surrender myself to you.

9   Rescue me from my enemies, O Lord,
> for I place myself under your protection.

10 Teach me to fulfill your purposes,
> for you are my God;
> may your Spirit of truth and love
> lead me to the world recreated to your design.

¹¹ Heal me, O Lord, to magnify your character of love;
    cleanse my soul from sinfulness, because you always do right.
¹² Show mercy to my enemies and let them go;
    let perish all those who reject healing and persist in attacking me,
    for I am your faithful follower. ☙

PSALM 144
HE IS MY SOURCE OF HEALING LOVE

¹ Praise the Lord, my Rock,
    who gives me strength for daily battles
    and the skill to be victorious in spiritual warfare;
² he is my source of healing love, my strength for right living,
    my shelter from life's storms and my remedy to sinfulness;
    my shield—the One I trust—
    who overcomes all my enemies.
³ O Lord, why are humans so important to you,
    or the Son of Man that you established a purpose for him?
⁴ Humans are like a puff of wind;
    their lives are short like a passing shadow.
⁵ O Lord, tear open the veil separating heaven and earth and come down;
    touch the mountains with your fiery presence enveloping them in smoke.
⁶ Send forth your lightning of love to scatter the selfish;
    send out your arrows of truth to destroy all who cling to lies.
⁷ Send your Right Hand down from heaven;
    rescue me from the sea of enemies—
    from the power of those who reject your kingdom of love,
⁸ those who speak only lies,
    who embrace the power of deceit.
⁹ I will sing my life-renewed as a song to you, O God;
    like a stringed instrument, my life will make music celebrating you,
¹⁰ the One who delivers kings,
    who rescued his servant David from evil's sword—

the infection of selfishness.
¹¹ Save me! Rescue me
>> from the power of those who reject your kingdom of love:
they speak only lies
>> and embrace the power of deceit.
¹² Then our sons will be like well-tended plants
>> who begin bearing spiritual fruit in their youth,
and our daughters will grow in strength and beauty of character
>> like beautiful pillars carved for a palace.
¹³ Then our treasure will be complete,
>> full of every good thing.
Our flocks will multiply by thousands—
>> even by tens of thousands—filling the pastures;
¹⁴ our cattle will grow strong and healthy;
>> no one will break through our walls,
no one will be taken captive,
>> and no cry of distress will be heard in our streets.
¹⁵ Happy and healthy are the people of whom this is true;
>> happy and healthy are the people whose God is the Lord. ⌘

PSALM 145

YOUR GOVERNANCE IS ETERNAL

¹ I will exalt you, my Creator God and Sovereign King;
>> I will praise your character of love for ever and ever.
² I will praise you every day
>> and exalt your character of love for ever and ever.
³ The greatness of the Lord is to be glorified;
>> his greatness is infinite—no one can plumb its depths.
⁴ Generation after generation will glory in what you have done;
>> they will tell of your power—the power of truth and love—
⁵ the glorious outflow of your majestic character of love.
>> Upon the wonderful manifestations of your methods I will meditate;
⁶ the mighty power of your infinite character of love I will revere,

and I will proclaim your greatness.
7   Remembrance of your great goodness will produce an overflow
    of joyful celebration of your character of love.
8   The Lord is gracious and compassionate, seeking to heal all;
    so rich in love, he is reluctant to let anyone go.
9   The Lord is good to all;
    he pours compassion on his entire creation.
10 All your works glorify you, O Lord;
    your friends honor and extol you.
11 They will tell of the glory of your kingdom of love
    and speak of your power—the power of infinite truth and love—
12 so that all people may know the power of your glorious presence
    and the beauty of your kingdom of love.
13 Your governance is eternal—an everlasting kingdom upon which life is built;
    your dominion sustains life through all generations.
    [The Lord's word is always reliable;
    his actions are always an expression of his character of love.] [16]
14 The Lord sustains those who fall
    and restores all those who humbly acknowledge their need.
15 Everyone considers you;
    you are the giver of food in due season.
16 You open your hand, giving freedom
    for every living thing to fulfill their desires.
17 The Lord is righteous in all his ways;
    the outworking of love in all he does.
18 The Lord enters into the closest intimacy with those who call on him,
    to all who call on him with hearts that love truth.
19 The Lord provides the desired remedy to all who trust and revere him;
    he gladly responds to their cry for help and heals them.
20 The Lord saves all who love him,
    but all those hardened in selfishness will perish.
21 I will praise the Lord forever.
    Let every living being praise his perfect character of love
    for ever and ever. ৎ

---

[16] Many ancient manuscripts do not include these last two lines (in parenthesis) of Psalm 145:13.

PSALM 146
THE LORD GIVES THE ABILITY TO SEE REALITY

1 Praise the Lord.
   I praise the Lord with my entire being.
2 I will praise the Lord by revealing his character of love in my life;
   I will make my life a song of praise to my God.
3 Do not put your trust in world leaders—
   humans, terminal in sin, who have no remedy to save and heal.
4 When their breath of life departs, they decay, returning to the dust;
   on that day their thoughts cease.
5 Happy and healthy are those whose help comes from the God of Jacob,
   who trust in the Lord their God—
6 the Designer, Creator and Sustainer of heaven and earth,
   the sea and all that is in them.
   The Lord preserves truth—the methods of love—forever.
7 He does what is right—he delivers the oppressed,
   dispensing the justice of love;
   he gives food to those who hunger,
   and those imprisoned by fear and selfishness he sets free.
8 To those blinded by Satan's lies, the Lord gives the ability to see reality;
   those who humble themselves, the Lord heals to everlasting life;
   the Lord's love fills those who are set right with him.
9 The Lord preserves those who are in this world but not of it;
   he is father to the fatherless and comforter to those who mourn,
   but he fills the way of wickedness with frustration,
   multiplying the opportunities to repent.
10 The Lord reigns forever;
   your God, O Zion, is everlasting.
   Praise the Lord. ❧

Psalm 147

He designed and sustains the circle of life

1   Praise the Lord.
    O how good it is to sing praises to our Creator God,
        how pleasant, beautiful and appropriate to praise him!
2   The Lord establishes his people;
        he brings his scattered children home.
3   He heals the brokenhearted
        and brings closure to their wounds.
4   He counts the stars
        and names each one of them.
5   Great is our Lord and absolute in power;
        his wisdom and understanding are infinite.
6   The Lord intervenes on behalf of those who humbly surrender to him,
        but those who refuse healing disintegrate back into the earth.
7   Sing thanks to the Lord;
        with stringed instruments, give praises to God.
8   He designed and sustains the circle of life:
        the clouds clothe the skies, bringing rain to the earth
        and providing water for grass to grow on the hills—
9   thus he feeds the cattle
        and the young ravens when they call for food.
10 He is not pleased by those who rely upon the power of war-horses
        or place their confidence in human strength;
11 the Lord delights in those who revere and rely upon him—
        who put their trust in his unfailing love.
12 Praise the Lord, you people of righteousness;
        praise your God, you citizens of his kingdom of love,
13 for he strengthens your resolve to resist evil
        and blesses all those who unite with you in love.
14 He brings healing and peace within your borders
        and satisfies you with the Bread of heaven.
15 He sends commands throughout the earth, that govern nature—
        his will instantaneously sustains its operation.
16 He permits snow to blanket the earth
        and frost to dust the land;

17 he allows hail to fall like crumbs.
      Who can stand against such cold?
18 At his direction, the seasons change and the ice melts;
      he brings the warm spring breezes, and snowmelt flows.
19 He has revealed his will to his people,
      his design-law and methods to those who unite with him and overcome.
20 He has not done this for the heathen—those who prefer selfishness;
      they do not know his laws—his designs of love, truth and liberty.
    Praise the Lord. ℘

PSALM 148

LET ALL THINGS GIVE PRAISE TO THE LORD'S CHARACTER OF LOVE

1 Praise the Lord.
   Praise the Lord from heaven,
      praise him from the expanse of the universe.
2 Praise the Lord, you loyal angels of God,
      praise him, all intelligent beings throughout the heavens.
3 Praise him, sun and moon,
      praise him, all you shining stars.
4 Praise him, you heaven of heavens
      and the waters above the sky.
5 Let all things give praise to the Lord's character of love,
      for at his command they were created.
6 He established them in their place for ever and ever;
      his design for life will never pass away.
7 Praise the Lord from the earth,
      you great creatures in the sea and all within the deepest ocean.
8 May all nature praise the Lord—lightning, hail, snow and clouds,
      stormy winds that fulfill his purposes,
9 the mountains and hills,
      fruit trees and cedars,
10 wild and domesticated animals,
      small creatures and flying birds,
11 rulers of the earth and all peoples,

princes and all leaders on earth,
12 young men and women,
old people and children.
13 May they all praise the Lord's character of love,
for his character alone is supreme;
his glory is superior to the earth and the heavens.
14 He has healed his people and made them strong in righteousness,
a people who glorify him in their characters—
united in heart with him, they overcome.
Praise the Lord. ☙

PSALM 149

HE HEALS HIS PEOPLE, CROWNING THE HUMBLE WITH ETERNAL LIFE

1 Praise the Lord.
Sing to the Lord a new heart-song,
sing his praise in the company of those who are renewed to be like him.
2 Let those, who with God, overcome
celebrate their unity with their Creator;
let the people of heaven's kingdom rejoice in their King.
3 Let them praise, with dancing, his character of love,
and accompanied by tambourine and harp, sing his praises.
4 For the Lord loves and enjoys his people;
he heals them, crowning the humble with eternal life.
5 Let the godly rejoice in their healing—their glorification—
singing for joy as they are finally at rest.
6 The exaltation of God is in their mouths
as they wield the power of the two-edged sword of truth
7 to defeat the lies and selfishness of the wicked
and rebuke the worldliness of the people,
8 binding their rulers with the chains of searing truth
and shackling their leaders with iron-clad reality,
9 to make known their terminal condition diagnosed against them.
The honor of wielding the truth is the privilege of all the healed.
Praise the Lord. ☙

Psalm 150

Praise him for the mighty things he has done

1 Praise the Lord.
   Praise God in his heavenly sanctuary;
      praise him in his infinite power of truth and love.
2 Praise him for the mighty things he has done;
      praise him for his supreme greatness.
3 Praise him with sounds of trumpet,
      praise him with harp and lyre,
4 praise him with tambourine and dancing,
      praise him with strings and flute,
5 praise him with resounding cymbals,
      praise him with the clash of cymbals.
6 Let every living thing praise the Lord.
   Praise the Lord! ०४०४०४

Come and Reason Ministries

is dedicated to helping you learn to discern, to stimulate you to think,
to help hone and refine your reasoning powers,
to increase your ability to know right from wrong and healthy from unhealthy.

We're not here to tell you what to think
but to show you how to more efficiently use your God-given reasoning power
to better grow in grace and experience a closer walk with God.

DISCOVER MORE!

Want to learn more about Come and Reason Ministries?

Visit us online today and get:

More Books by Dr. Jennings

Blogs on Current Topics • Podcasts • Seminars • Bible Study Guides

Answers to Difficult Bible Questions • Weekly Bible Study Class

Life-transforming information on

Christian growth ▫ Bible principles for better mental health ▫
healthier families and relationships ▫ strengthening the mind and body ▫
human sexuality, and so much more!

Find it all at
comeandreason.com

Also find us on
Facebook, YouTube, Instagram